HALF FULL

An Interpretive Guide to Proverbs

BY
A. WENDELL BOWES

f▸

THE FOUNDRY
PUBLISHING®

The Foundry Publishing®
PO Box 419527
Kansas City, MO 64141
thefoundrypublishing.com

ISBN 978-0-8341-4322-7

Cover design: Caines Design
Interior design: Sharon Page

Library of Congress Cataloging-in-Publication Data
A complete catalog record for this book is available from the Library of Congress.

To
Simon and Johonah,
may you always live lives of goodness and wisdom
guided by the Sages' advice
in Proverbs and Ecclesiastes.

Not only was the Teacher wise, but he also imparted knowledge to the people.
He pondered and searched out and set in order many proverbs.
The Teacher searched to find just the right words, and what he wrote was upright and true.
—Ecclesiastes 12:9-10

Half Full and its companion volume, *Half Empty,* were published following the author's early and unexpected death. His family is pleased to share Wendell's last words of wisdom with you.

CONTENTS

Preface   7

Abbreviations   11

Introduction   13
    Preliminary Considerations   14
    Introductory Sermon   19

  I. **Introduction and Theme: How to Be Successful
     and Wise (Prov. 1:1–7)**   27
    The Superscription   27
    The Purposes of Proverbs   28
    Most Importantly, Encourage People to Fear the Lord   32
    What Can We Learn from These Few Verses?   34

 II. **Instructions (Prov. 1:8–9:18)**   37
    Peer Pressure   37
    Lady Wisdom Is Looking for You   42
    Not All Fools Are the Same   46
    Wisdom's Rewards   51
    Friends and Neighbors   58
    Lady Foolishness Has Her Eyes on You   65
    Lady Wisdom's Remarkable Character and Usefulness   72
    Fight of the Ages   80

III. **Individual Sayings Attributed to Solomon
     (Prov. 10:1–22:16)**   85
    Advice for Children   85
    Let's Hear It for Common Sense   92
    The Power of the Tongue   102
    A Good Marriage   110
    What's in a Name?   116
    Advice for Parents   123

IV. Thirty "Sayings of the Wise" (Prov. 22:17—24:22)   131
    Don't Move Those Stones!   131

V. Additional "Sayings of the Wise" (Prov. 24:23-34)   138
    Laziness   138

VI. More Sayings Attributed to Solomon, Which Hezekiah Preserved (Prov. 25:1—29:27)   144
    The Paradoxes of Life   144

VII. Sayings Attributed to Agur (Prov. 30:1-33)   154
    Never Enough!   155

VIII. Sayings Attributed to King Lemuel (Prov. 31:1-9)   160
    Order in the Court   161

IX. The Virtuous Woman (Prov. 31:10-31)   171
    A Woman to Be Praised   171

X. Additional Sermon Ideas from Proverbs   183
    The Importance of Knowledge   183
    Making Plans for the Future   183
    God's Judgment/Justice   184
    How to Treat the Poor   184
    Guidelines for Leaders   184
    Dealing with Enemies   184

References   185

PREFACE

I started this book and its companion volume on Ecclesiastes after writing *The Wisdom Literature* (Bowes 2024). In the process of my research for that book, I discovered that the resources for preaching from Proverbs and Ecclesiastes were extremely limited. Some commentators even discouraged trying to produce such resources. I accepted that as a challenge and began writing.

In hindsight, I probably bit off more than I could chew. Writing on Proverbs was a delight. So many topics in this book beg for consideration. It is a very practical guidebook for successful living. But Ecclesiastes was more difficult. I really struggled to find material that would be appropriate for the pulpit. The sermon resources I developed are worthy of consideration, but the effort was challenging. I hope preachers and teachers find my sermon-starter proposals helpful and will make the effort to use these biblical books in their ministry.

While driving around my community, I recently found myself following a car with a decal on its rear window: "Life Is Good." I wanted to stop the driver and learn the reasons for her optimism. But not wanting to be mistaken for a stalker, I instead began to ponder in my own mind whether I could make the same evaluation about my own life. I can honestly say that life overall has been good to me. Yes, there have been times of great distress and frustration. There have been times of financial concern. There have been times of sorrow and grief. I imagine there will be more such times in the years ahead. But overall, life is good. Physically, I am still kicking, but at a much slower pace. Intellectually, my mind still functions fairly well.

The titles of these two volumes (*Half Full* and *Half Empty*) attempt to highlight the major differences in people's outlooks on life. These differences are nowhere more evident than in the books of Proverbs and Ecclesiastes. The authors of both books were seeking the same goal—to find the meaning of life and to enable them to live successfully. They used the same resources in their research—observations of nature and human behavior, insights passed down from previous generations of sages, and instructions from God. Interestingly, these authors came to very different conclusions. In doing so, they illustrate the differences in how people look at life today.

The authors and collectors who created *Proverbs* were able to look on the bright side of life, emphasizing the good things they saw around them and the blessings God provides those who serve him. They were optimistic because they believed life would always go well for those who fear God (Prov. 11:27). They produced and preserved sayings that were happy and confident about life lived in God's will.

In contrast, the author and editor of *Ecclesiastes* were troubled by life's problems and senselessness. They had seen too many instances of bad things happening to good people. They were troubled by God's silence when people most needed him to make sense of their experiences. They felt they were wandering in a dark wilderness because they could not find the key to life's meaning. Consequently, they skeptically questioned whether any human being could ever understand the overall purpose of life. To them, life was not good; life was just vanity.

Such differences in perspective are still evident today. Many people have an optimistic mindset. Others, including believers, are constantly pessimistic. Such differences may be due to personality traits and upbringing. At other times, they are caused by differences in life's experiences. Imagine how inexplicable tragedies can turn people's lives topsy-turvy—dealing with the senseless death of a child in a school mass shooting, having to place a spouse in a memory-care facility, losing one's life savings to an identity thief. Such people would probably claim that life had not been good to them. They might feel they were living under a shadow that never went away.

Whatever the cause, we need to evaluate where we stand on the scale of optimism versus pessimism. We may need to make some adjustments or course corrections. We all want to live a good life. We all want to be successful in our families, our jobs, and our relationships.

We all want to enjoy good health and good finances. But sometimes our basic approach to life is overly optimistic (Proverbs) or overly pessimistic (Ecclesiastes). We fail to see life realistically, if we do not see it as God sees it.

Qohelet, the author of Ecclesiastes, had it about right when he encouraged his students to follow the golden mean—the middle pathway between the extremes (Eccles. 7:15-18). Somewhere in the middle is where he thought people should live. Modern culture would profit from that message.

The people in ancient times who produced the biblical canon have sometimes been criticized for including a book like Ecclesiastes. Its critics say it is simply too skeptical for Christians to read. They want people always to think positive thoughts, like those in Proverbs. But maybe the ancients were wiser than we give them credit for being. They certainly knew that Proverbs would be a popular book because it promises rewards to everyone who follows its advice. They also knew that life has its dark moments, when the sun disappears for days, weeks, months, even years at a time. Sometimes confusion and despair bring us to a crisis of faith. Saints have called such times the "dark night of the soul" (following John of the Cross).

Ecclesiastes offers a much-needed corrective to unrealistic optimism. It speaks to these darker moments and honestly asks questions that need to be considered. Therefore, wisely, the ancients included it in the canon alongside Proverbs. Hopefully, preachers and teachers today will follow their lead and include both these books in their preaching schedule. We all need to hear the profound messages that Proverbs and Ecclesiastes have provided people over the centuries.

—Wendell Bowes

ABBREVIATIONS

General

→	see another part of the book at
AD	anno Domini (precedes date)
ANE	ancient Near East(ern)
BC	before Christ (follows date)
c.	century
ca.	*circa*, around
cf.	compare
ch(s).	chapter(s)
ed(s).	editor(s); edition
e.g.	*exempli gratia*, for example
esp.	especially
etc.	*et cetera*, and the rest
HB	Hebrew Bible
ibid.	*ibidem*, in the same place
i.e.	*id est*, in other words, that is
l(l).	line(s)
lit.	literally
no(s).	number(s)
NT	New Testament
OT	Old Testament
trans.	translated by
v(v).	verse(s)
vol(s).	volume(s)

Modern English Bible Translations

AT	author's translation
GNT	Good News Translation (Today's English Version)
MSG	The Message
NASB	New American Standard Bible
NIV	New International Version (2011 ed.)
NJPS	Tanakh: The Holy Scriptures: The New Jewish Publication Society Translation
NRSV	New Revised Standard Version
Phillips	*The New Testament in Modern English* (J. B. Phillips)
TLB	The Living Bible

Modern Reference Works

ABD   *Anchor Bible Dictionary* (see Freedman)

AEL   *Ancient Egyptian Literature: A Book of Readings* (see Lichtheim)

ANET   *Ancient Near Eastern Texts Relating to the Old Testament* (see
             Pritchard)

INTRODUCTION

The fascinating collection of books known as the OT wisdom literature (Job, Proverbs, Ecclesiastes, and Song of Songs) is often bypassed in preachers' sermon schedules. Admittedly, these books are difficult to preach from. Job is a literary masterpiece with an imaginative storyline and an attractive and relevant topic. But the story drags on repetitively for forty-two chapters. Ecclesiastes puts off many readers because of its author's pessimism. The collection of love poetry in the Song of Songs seems more relevant for weddings than for Sunday morning worship.

The main problem with Proverbs is its lack of context. The book contains hundreds of short, instructive sayings that jump from topic to topic. Only rarely do two verses in a row deal with the same topic. This invites all kinds of misinterpretations and makes it difficult to serve as the basis for a cohesive series of sermons. One commentator observed, "Proverbs . . . do not readily provide inspiration or excitement. With the exception of Leviticus, it is doubtful that any biblical book is viewed with less enthusiasm by the preacher" (Collins 1980, 1). Although I disagree with that sentiment, the view probably resonates with many preachers. Reading *Preaching Proverbs: Wisdom for the Pulpit* by Alyce M. McKenzie (1996) might change their minds.

Even so, most Christians are familiar with parts of Proverbs. They have probably heard a Mother's Day sermon based on Proverbs 31:10-31. Daily devotional books may have introduced them to passages such as Proverbs 1:7; 3:5-6; 15:1, 29; 16:25; and 22:1. Preachers know that some in their congregations are somewhat acquainted with the book.

The challenge of using Proverbs in preaching and teaching is to find ways to build sermons out of a single verse and make it relevant to a contemporary congregation. It is a difficult but not impossible task. In this book, we look at one way to do that effectively. Here is some general information to keep in mind as we begin the process of developing a text from Proverbs into a sermon.

Preliminary Considerations

Allow me to repeat some general principles I suggested in my earlier book on preaching and teaching from the book of Job (Bowes 2021, 14-18).

1. Invest in Some Good Commentaries

A good library of resources is essential for constructing effective sermons and lessons. Ideally, one should have five or six commentaries on hand for each biblical book. These should include at least one that is theological in nature and one that focuses on accurately translating and interpreting the Hebrew text. The volumes by Clifford, Fox (two vols.), Hartley, Kidner, Longman, and Waltke (two vols.) are especially helpful. See the list of references at the end of the book for further suggestions.

2. Make Use of Several Different Bible Versions That Employ Different Theories of Translation

Bible translations seem to be a problem for some pastors, so here are some comments to help resolve the confusion. There are many good versions of the Bible on the market today. Laypeople are often perplexed about which to buy for themselves or as a gift for a family member. Too often, decisions are based on the color or quality of the cover. When asked, I usually encourage people to tell me what is important to them in choosing a Bible. The following are some questions that need to be answered first.

a. What Are You Going to Use the Bible For?

Is this a Bible for devotional reading? For writing sermons and college term papers? For a Bible study group? For memorization? Or is this a gift for your elementary child or teenager? There are versions appropriate for every use.

b. How Literal a Translation Do You Want?

Are you looking for a literal translation that is as close to the original Hebrew and Greek texts as possible? A contemporary translation that uses modern language and grammar? A completely free version that attempts to convey ideas clearly rather than accurately rendering individual words? Some paraphrases of the Bible have not consulted the original Hebrew and Greek.

c. With What English Format Are You Comfortable?

There was almost no formatting in the original biblical texts. Modern versions attempt to make translations more user friendly in appearance. Do you want distinctions made between poetry and prose sections? Do you want inserted editorial headings and paragraph divisions? Capitalized pronouns referring to God? The words of Jesus in red?

d. How Do You Want to Read Weights, Measures, Monetary Units, and Calendar Designations?

Are you happy with the original Hebrew words such as "shekels," "talents," "cubits," "homers," and months like "Nisan"? Or would you prefer conversions into English equivalents such as "dollars," "pounds," "kilograms," "inches," "meters," "quarts," and months like "April"? Regarding modern monetary units, readers must be aware that these change over time because of inflation.

e. How Do You Prefer the Version to Treat Words Referring to Sexual Parts of the Body and Bathroom Activities?

Would you rather that your Bible contain a euphemism or a word that is accurate but graphic? Compare Genesis 31:35 in the NRSV and NIV for an example of each.

f. How Do You Want the Version to Treat Gendered Language?

Many translations today use plural pronouns (such as "they," "them," "themselves") in texts that refer to all people, not just males. But the plural changes the reference to the number of people mentioned. For example, compare the more literal rendering of Mark 4:25 in the NASB with the gender-neutral rendering in the NRSV.

g. *Does It Matter If the Version Was Translated by a Committee or an Individual?*

Most versions were translated by a select committee of biblical scholars, but a few (such as The Message, *The New Testament in Modern English* [Phillips], and The Living Bible) were crafted by one person. Theological biases are more apt to appear in a single-person translation.

h. *Do You Want Only the Printed Biblical Text, or Do You Want the Additional Resources Provided by Study Bibles?*

Study Bibles include maps, notes at the foot of each page, and explanations at the beginning of each book. They also usually include cross-references to quotations and possible allusions in other biblical passages.

As you think about the Bible versions that you are going to use in sermon or lesson preparation, be aware that no one translation perfectly satisfies all your wishes. Each has strengths and weaknesses. Therefore, choose several translations that offer a wide variety of renderings of each text.

The versions I turn to most frequently are the NRSV (fairly literal), GNT (free), NIV (dynamically equivalent), and the NJPS (Jewish). The translators of each version used a different set of principles to guide their translations. That is refreshing and helpful.

3. Allow Yourself Adequate Time for Preparation

I admit to preparing a few sermons late on Saturday night. They were not my best. Good preaching from any biblical book requires sufficient preparation. Proverbs is no exception. In fact, it may require more preparation because of its unique nature.

The main challenge to using Proverbs in sermons is figuring out what a one-verse text means and then to expand the context by including other proverbs or passages to build a solid base of biblical support. It takes time to trace down other relevant proverbs and to construct an outline that deals with the larger scriptural context. Some commentaries helpfully bring multiple proverbs together on a single theme: Aitken (1986, 93-252), Goldingay (2014, 157-75), Kidner (1964, 31-56, 185-92), Longman (2006, 549-78), and Scott (1965, 130-31, 171). Pippert's *Words from the Wise* (2003) rearranges the book of

Proverbs by word and theme. When using multiple passages in sermons, you can help your congregations follow along if you prepare presentation slides for each passage you discuss.

Another daunting task in preaching from Proverbs is to determine how a proverb may apply to a contemporary setting. Ancient proverbs were written to apply to specific situations, under certain conditions. Their short format leaves no room for considering every possible situation or exception. It takes time for preachers to uncover the exceptions (sometimes in another proverb or biblical book) and to decide how best to acknowledge them in the sermon or lesson.

It also takes time to find good illustrations. There are people in every congregation whom Proverbs would label fools. As their pastor, you would like to grab them by the lapels and shout at them to wake up. They are headed toward spiritual disaster. Of course, you cannot do that. However, sometimes a good illustration can be as effective as a slap on the face in getting them to see themselves from God's viewpoint. A biblical example such as Saul, Jonah, or Jacob is always appropriate. For other sermons, a character in a TV sitcom or well-known novel can be effective. People you have known while growing up or in college can also illustrate a sermon. In any case, you need time to allow the Holy Spirit to remind you of appropriate illustrations to make your sermon relevant to your congregation.

4. Take Advantage of the Timeless Nature of the Wisdom Books

All the wisdom books are timeless in nature. Job forces us to think about unjust suffering. Ecclesiastes challenges us with trying to find meaning in a world that often is unfair, contradictory, and unexplainable. Proverbs gives us insights into how to live well. These are basic human issues that transcend time, geography, race, and gender. They are just as relevant today as when they were first written. This timelessness provides preachers and teachers with a multitude of fascinating topics.

5. Plan to Preach a Series of Sermons from Proverbs over Several Months

I often told ministerial students that if they really want their congregation to know the Bible, they must spend a meaningful amount of time on each book. Congregations will never come to understand

Proverbs with just a single sermon every few years. They need a sermon series that explains the overall purpose of the book and develops its major themes. To teach your congregation effectively, plan a series over several months. Such preaching is real biblical preaching.

In the Northern Hemisphere, late fall, winter, and spring are usually dedicated to the major liturgical seasons in the church calendar centered on Christmas and Easter. However, summertime provides a more relaxed atmosphere when families are out of school and on vacation. This creates the perfect opportunity to preach a series of sermons on the happy little sayings in Proverbs. There is no storyline, allowing preachers to jump from chapter to chapter, picking texts that are appropriate and enlightening. In addition, worshippers who go on vacation will not miss some important segment in the story, as would happen with Job or the narrative sections of the OT. Bible study groups will find Proverbs profitable any time of the year.

One approach to preaching a series from Proverbs is to announce ahead of time that the sermons for the next several months will focus on the OT's guidebook for successful living. Everyone would like to know how to be wise. Everyone wants to be a good friend or neighbor. Everyone would appreciate some good advice on how to pick a spouse and how to raise their children. Everyone would like to know how to say the right thing at the right time. Everyone has crossed paths with fools and wondered how to deal with them. All of these topics are covered in the book of Proverbs. "So," preachers can say, "plan to be in church as many Sundays as you can during the next few months because all of these topics will be addressed."

One of the most popular sections of Proverbs is the chapter that deals with the virtuous woman (Prov. 31:10-31). It is frequently used as a sermon text on Mother's Day. Because of this, it could be an appropriate text to begin a summer series.

There are literally dozens of topics in the book of Proverbs that could be addressed from the pulpit or in the classroom. I have chosen twenty-two to give preachers an idea of how to go about it. There is at least one from every collection within the book. These are not full sermon manuscripts; they need to be expanded with illustrations and further explanations. Nevertheless, there is ample material here to provide several months of sermons. May both you and your congregation benefit from spending some quality time in the book of Proverbs.

6. A Word to Teachers

I wrote these two volumes to encourage pastors to preach more sermons from Proverbs and Ecclesiastes. However, I would also like to challenge Sunday school teachers and Bible study group leaders to tackle these two wisdom books. There are many, many topics in these books that could profitably be addressed in a teacher-student format. May your faith be strengthened and your knowledge increased as you seek to uncover some of the Bible's best instructions on successful living.

Introductory Sermon

Probably the best way to begin a series of sermons on the book of Proverbs is to define what we mean by a proverb. A biblical proverb is *a short, didactic saying stating a truth about human existence from God's point of view.* There are 915 of these short sayings in the book of Proverbs. Some appear in groups that focus on a common theme, such as wisdom, folly, adultery, or the virtuous woman. They instruct readers in how to understand a specific issue in life and how to direct their behavior in response. Still, hundreds of others are not arranged in any logical format. They are just randomly strung together.

There are several characteristics of proverbial sayings and the book of Proverbs itself. It is important to consider these when beginning a series of sermons from this practical book. A fuller explanation can be found in my book *The Wisdom Literature* (Bowes 2024, 92-101).

1. Proverbs Are Very Old

Archaeologists have discovered collections of proverbs in both Mesopotamia and Egypt that date back to at least 2700 BC. That is eighteen hundred years before Solomon, who is credited as the most prolific proverb writer of Israel. The Bible mentions several areas in the ancient Near East (ANE) that were known for their wisdom sayings. They included Mesopotamia and Egypt (1 Kings 4:29-31), Phoenicia (Ezek. 27:8-9; 28:4-5), and Edom (Job 2:11; Jer. 49:7; Obad. 8).

The proverbs that have survived from these other ancient countries resemble biblical proverbs in both form and content. For example, one from about 1500 BC in Mesopotamia is similar to Proverbs 3:29 and reinforced by Jesus in the Sermon on the Mount (Matt. 5:38-42):

Do not return evil to your adversary;
Requite with kindness the one who does evil to you. (*ANET*, 595, ll. 41-42)

Interest in proverbial sayings was a universal phenomenon in the ancient world. The biblical sages acknowledged this by borrowing the forms of the wisdom literature from other countries as well as preserving many of their ideas. Solomon may have had his scribes secure copies of wisdom collections from other countries.

2. Proverbs Are Popular

By popular, we do not mean that they have a huge fan club. We mean that they are intended for the use of the general public, average people, not specialists. Human civilization has always been attracted to proverbial sayings. Parents want to teach their children the basic values and beliefs necessary for success in a particular culture. Proverbs do this easily because they are short enough and catchy enough to be memorized even by young children.

Most cultures that have ever existed have created proverbial sayings. North American culture is no exception: "Better late than never," and "Don't count your chickens before they hatch." Benjamin Franklin is especially revered as a collector and creator of American proverbs through his pamphlet *Poor Richard's Almanack* (1732-58). A well-known German proverb is, "Es gibt kein schlechtes Wetter, nur falsche Kleidung." (There is no such thing as bad weather, only the wrong clothing.) A famous African proverb is, "If you want to go fast, go alone; if you want to go far, go together."

The popularity of wisdom sayings in NT times is illustrated by Jesus's continual use of wisdom forms in his teaching. Witherington estimates that at least 70 percent of Jesus's teachings in the Gospels are in the form of wisdom sayings—aphorisms, riddles, and parables (1994, 155-56). Thus he purposely "intended to be seen, at least in part, as some kind of sage" (155). This is further confirmed in his word to the scribes and Pharisees that his wisdom was even greater than Solomon's (Matt. 12:42).

Proverbial sayings are still popular today. We hear and read them all the time—in media advertising, on billboards, in songs, and in political slogans. New proverbs are created every year. Modern speakers often use proverbs "to illustrate a statement, to clinch an argument, or to lend authority to an admonition" (Scott 1965, 3).

3. Most Proverbs Were Originally Oral and Anonymous

The book of Proverbs was not produced by a single author. It is a collection of smaller collections of Israel's best wisdom sayings. These sayings were probably spoken first. Later, they were written down and placed in collections. An editor or editors established the final form of the book later still, at least two hundred years after Solomon. Proverbs 25:1 mentions the participation of Judah's king Hezekiah in this process. Apparently, the final editors attempted to keep each small collection together as a whole, for they did not eliminate sayings in one collection that were identical or similar to those in another. Neither did they attempt to organize the book by subject matter. Consequently, the topic of an individual proverb is often strikingly different from those on either side.

It is impossible to date the origin of any single saying within Proverbs since there is no historical information within them. King Solomon is credited with writing many of these proverbs, but there were other authors, including professional sages and ordinary Israelites and Judeans. In most biblical books, the date and authorship are crucial pieces of evidence for interpretation. The identification of the various authors in Proverbs though is merely a matter of curiosity. It is not crucial to interpretation. Thus preachers and teachers need not be concerned with identifying these elements. The topics in Proverbs are universal, timeless, and relevant, no matter when they were produced.

4. The Structure of the Book Is Based on Its Collections

For some unknown reason, the organization of the book of Proverbs follows the order of the smaller collections with the addition of editorial headings:

1:1-7	Introduction and Theme
1:8–9:18	Instructions
10:1–22:16	Individual Sayings Attributed to Solomon

22:17–24:22	Thirty "Sayings of the Wise"
24:23-34	Additional "Sayings of the Wise"
25:1–29:27	More Sayings Attributed to Solomon, Which Hezekiah Preserved
30:1-33	Sayings Attributed to Agur
31:1-9	Sayings Attributed to King Lemuel
31:10-31	The Virtuous Woman

5. The Underlying Theme of Biblical Proverbs Is God's Established Order

In all biblical Proverbs, an underlying theme is that God established order in the world at the time of creation. Everything that was created fits in an appropriate place that God designed for it. This order can be seen most readily in the natural world, such as in the orderly and regular paths the sun, moon, and stars take across the heavens; the orderly progression of the seasons; and the orderly habits of the animal kingdom as seen in living habits, reproductive behavior, and migration. These all demonstrate that the Creator established order in his world.

God also intended for there to be order in human behavior and social interactions between people. Our attitudes, speech, and actions are among the subjects regularly addressed in Proverbs.

Finally, there is order in the world of morality. Certain activities and attitudes are right from God's point of view, and others are wrong. God intended for humans to be righteous, self-disciplined, honest, good children, good spouses, good friends and neighbors. And they should especially be wise. God also intended for humans to avoid wickedness, deceit, foolishness, and laziness. Human beings should figure out what these activities are and live their lives accordingly (for additional comments on the order that God planned for creation, → the sermon "Order in the Court," p. 161).

This concept of order applies to all areas of life, even to areas we might label as "secular." For example, Proverbs 12:11 speaks to the issue of good work habits:

Those who work their land will have abundant food,
but those who chase fantasies have no sense.

Proverbs 15:1 points out the importance of good speech:

A gentle answer turns away wrath,
> but a harsh word stirs up anger.

Neither of these proverbs has any obviously *religious* content. They appear to be simply commonsense principles that are completely secular. Israel viewed them as religious and included them in the book of Proverbs because they describe an area of life that God has ordered. To write about this order is to enlighten people on the way God intended for life to operate.

Proverbs is probably the most pragmatic book in the OT. It assumes that we all want to live successful lives, and so it gives us wise and godly advice on all kinds of practical topics, such as our marriage, our family, our speech, our friends and neighbors, and differences between wise people and fools. In each of these areas, Proverbs tells us what to do and what to avoid. It wants to share with us "the way life actually works" (Goldingay 2014, 4) or *should* work.

Sometimes we may regard the topics in Proverbs as too mundane and ordinary to be of interest to God. But the sages viewed life differently. They believed that nothing is too insignificant to be outside of God's planned order for this world. As Brueggemann notes, for the sages "daily life is morally serious and urgent." Further, "daily life is inescapably linked to the structure of creation willed by the creator. Because of that linkage, even our most mundane actions and decisions are permeated with moral thickness that we cannot avoid" (2019, 154). Thus we need good advice on ordering our lives according to God's desires. The book of Proverbs is our guidebook to do this.

The method Proverbs uses for its guidance is "moral persuasion" (Witherington 1994, 26). The sages were not preachy or confrontational like the prophets. They did not need to be; the truth was self-evidently on their side. Their precepts had been proven true over centuries. For the sages, it just made good sense to fit in with the order God had already established in the world.

6. To Understand God's Order in the World, One Must Become Wise

The OT viewed wisdom as "a proper understanding of human existence as viewed from God's perspective and the living out of that understanding in one's own personal life (Ps. 111:10)" (Bowes 2024,

21). How does one gain this wisdom about human existence? The sages used three sources to gain this wisdom, and we can too.

First, they observed the natural world and human behavior over a long time. Much can be learned by just silently observing what is going on around oneself.

Second, they learned from the teachings of previous generations of sages. Wisdom writings began in the ANE as early as 2700 BC, so there was a long tradition of wisdom principles from which Israelite sages could draw. In essence, the book of Proverbs is a collection of teachings that have been drawn from the wisdom of many generations.

Third, the sages sought God's guidance. Since God had created the world and ordered its operations, he naturally knew more about how it ought to run than anyone else. This is reflected in the theme verse of Proverbs (1:7) as well as other passages (Job 12:13; 28:28; Ps. 111:10; Prov. 2:1-6; 9:10; Hos. 14:9 [10 HB]). People today set all kinds of goals for themselves—in personal relationships, in business, in education, in finances, and so on. According to the sages, human efforts will probably fail if we neglect God's guidance. The book of Proverbs calls such people "fools" (Prov. 1:7).

Before concluding this sermon, we should note that wisdom is just as significant a topic in the NT as it is in the Old. The Greek words for "wisdom" (*sophia*), "wise" (*sophos*), and "make wise" (*sophizō*) appear over seventy times in the NT. Several key thoughts arise from these verses.

First, wisdom is an attribute of God (Luke 11:49).

Second, God's wisdom is identified with and embodied in Jesus Christ (Luke 2:40; 1 Cor. 1:24, 30; Col. 2:2-3).

Third, God's wisdom is extremely valuable because it is far greater than that of human beings (Rom. 11:33-36; 1 Cor. 1:25).

Fourth, God's wisdom has been and continues to be conveyed to human beings through the teachings of the Holy Spirit (1 Cor. 2:6-7, 12-13; Eph. 1:8*b*-10; Col. 1:9). God encourages us to ask for it (James 1:5).

Fifth, God wants all human beings to live lives of wisdom (Eph. 5:15-17). Such lives are characterized by "righteousness, holiness and redemption" (1 Cor. 1:30). Wise people live in humility, seeking to be "pure . . . peace-loving, considerate, submissive, full of mercy and good fruit, impartial and sincere" (James 3:17; see vv. 13-18).

These five key thoughts are at the heart of what God is asking each of us today: Do you want to be wise? Have you asked God to give you wisdom, as Solomon did at the beginning of his reign (1 Kings 3:4-15)? Have you allowed God's wisdom to shape your life by reverencing the Lord (Prov. 1:7) and asking Christ to forgive you of your sins (1 Cor. 1:30)? Are you trying to live a life of wisdom as described by Paul in 1 Corinthians 1:30 and by James in James 3:13-18?

Possible Sermon Titles: "Guidebook to Successful Living," "God's Textbook," "A Significant Word from Israel's Sages"

I. INTRODUCTION AND THEME: HOW TO BE SUCCESSFUL AND WISE (PROV. 1:1-7)

Proverbs 1:1-7 is a short introduction to the entire book. The final editor(s) placed it here to give readers some insight into the contents of the book. Four topics are mentioned in these verses:

- The connection of the book to King Solomon (v. 1).
- The importance of gaining wisdom about life (vv. 2-6).
- The two groups who need to read this book: those who lack wisdom—specifically, the simple and the young (v. 4), and those who already have wisdom but need further instructions (v. 5).
- The most important principle for gaining wisdom: Fear the Lord (v. 7). Without this first step, one's search for wisdom will be futile.

This short section of verses provides an introduction to the book. This makes it ideally suited for introducing a series of sermons based on the book.

The Superscription (Prov. 1:1)

To understand verse 1, the reader needs to be aware of ancient literary practices. Most books in the ANE, including the OT, were originally anonymous. The final editor(s) sometimes added superscriptions to aid readers in making a connection with a specific author (e.g., Eccles. 1:1; Song of Sol. 1:1; Isa. 1:1; Jer. 1:1-3; Hos. 1:1, etc.). The first verse in Proverbs is such a superscription. Certainly, the creator of the superscription was aware that the book was composed of several small collections by different authors. But tying the book to Solomon gave it authority and challenged people to read its contents. Who would not want to read a book connected with one of Israel's greatest and wisest kings?

Advertisers today often do something similar in trying to sell their products, and we think nothing of it. Well-known people in sports, entertainment, and business often appear in commercials to sell us cars, electronic devices, and toothpaste. If, as widely thought, the sages were instrumental in compiling this book, they certainly would have been interested in using Solomon's reputation for wisdom to promote this book. This was one way they could influence their society with a worldview that stressed order, right behavior, and obedience to God.

The Purposes of Proverbs (Prov. 1:2-6)

Verses 2-6 were also created by the final editor(s) to state the overall purpose of the entire book. Notice the number of nouns and verbs in this passage that refer to instruction and learning. They indicate that the book was designed as a textbook about life. These words are prominent throughout the wisdom literature, so it is important that we spend some time trying to understand their meaning before trying to construct a sermon. These verses state five purposes for the book of Proverbs and identify two audiences that will find the book helpful in life.

1. Learn Wisdom and Discipline (Prov. 1:2a)

The word "wisdom" (*ḥokmâ*) was defined earlier in the introduction to the book. It refers to "a proper understanding of human existence as viewed from God's perspective and the living out of that understanding in one's own personal life" (→ introduction, p. 23). Wisdom, then, applies both to a body of knowledge and to the application of that knowledge to daily living. It is right thinking and right living, and the central tenet of all this is "the fear of the LORD" (1:7).

"Discipline" (AT; *mûsār*) refers to the instructions and corrections that loving parents impose on their children (22:15) or that a loving God imposes on those who fear him (Job 5:17). When parents discipline their children, they usually include instructions on ways to do better or behaviors to avoid. However, there may also be chastening and punishment concerning bad conduct. The basic meaning of *mûsār* is not just simple instructions, but rather instructions with "correction, whether by verbal rebuke or by physical punishment" (Fox 2000, 34). The intended result of this discipline is the improvement of one's moral character and the incorporation of wise principles into one's life. Those who accept this discipline willingly and learn from it will become better people; those who reject it are just plain stupid (Prov. 12:1). For the NT perspective on the necessity of God's discipline, see Hebrews 12:4-13.

Therefore, one reason to read the book of Proverbs is to gain a correct understanding of life and to receive the discipline and correction needed to live according to this understanding.

2. Understand Words of Insight (Prov. 1:2*b*)

"Words of insight" (*bînâ*) refers to the instructions needed to gain wisdom. These instructions could refer generally to the entire body of wisdom principles taught by the sages. However, the location of this phrase in the introduction to the book is clearly an encouragement to use especially the sayings in Proverbs as a learning resource for gaining wisdom. A person needs to understand the words of this book to become wise. Thus reading Proverbs and comprehending its message are important components in becoming wise.

A good understanding is more than just memorizing the book of Proverbs. It requires comprehending how wisdom fits into the larger scheme of life God has ordered according to his desires. Proverbs is convinced that it can teach us the true nature of wisdom, both its "substance" and its "expression" (Waltke 2004, 174). Its hundreds of sayings increase our understanding of what wisdom is, how it may be acquired, how it is to be lived out, and how to recognize it in others. Proverbs also indicates that there are other resources for gaining wisdom, including God, "Lady Wisdom," parents, wise teachers, the reasoning processes of the mind, life experiences, and comparative lessons from the animal kingdom and nature.

3. Acquire the Moral Discipline to Become Wise (Prov. 1:3)

The literal translation of verse 3*a* is "for acquiring the discipline of insight/understanding" (AT; *haśkēl*). It means "to absorb" the corrections that Proverbs teaches us and to make them a part of our lives (Fox 2000, 59). The second half of verse 3, then, enlarges on the areas of teaching that need to be incorporated into our lives: "righteousness, justice, and equity" (NRSV). "Righteousness" (ṣedeq) means living in conformity to the will of God. It means knowing and practicing right order and behavior from God's perspective. "Justice" (mišpāṭ) refers to the right standards by which God judges the world. He expects all human beings to conform to these standards. "Equity" (mêšārîm; lit., "straightness," "uprightness") is a term generally used to describe speech or judgments that are true, honest, just, and fair.

All these are moral terms. They indicate that one's progress toward becoming wise must always include the development of a moral conscience that guides one's thinking and actions toward others. Character formation was always an important goal in the sages' teachings.

4. Teach Shrewdness, Knowledge, and Discretion to the Simple and the Young (Prov. 1:4)

The "simple" (pətî/pətā'yîm) are naive (22:3; 27:12); they live in an unrealistic, fantasy world (12:11). They just wander through life with no understanding of its purpose or application to them. Their lack of self-discipline leaves them unprepared for temptations, disasters, and complex issues in life (7:6-27). They are headed for an early death (1:32). These are not necessarily young children who have never been to school. They could be teens and adults who have had plenty of opportunities to learn the ways of wisdom but have ignored or rejected all offers.

It is vitally important that simpleminded people grow up mentally. To do so, they need to be educated. They need to gain "knowledge" (da'at). Moreover, they also need to learn how to use that knowledge to make good decisions that demonstrate forethought, planning, "shrewdness" (AT; 'ormâ), and "discretion" (məzimmâ). This is especially important for those who have been naively drifting along in life without a sense of direction or purpose. The simpleminded man in Proverbs 7:6-27 illustrates the tragedy that awaits those who never grow up. They easily yield to temptations and suffer the consequences. They are on a road that leads "to the grave" (v. 27).

The mention of "the young" highlights the concern of Proverbs to educate the next generation in the ways of wisdom. Repeatedly, we find admonitions addressed to "my son" (1:8, 10; 2:1; etc.). Even the well-known passage on the virtuous woman (31:10-31) was probably written to help young men choose a good wife. No specific age is attached to the word "young." It seems to indicate the years between birth and early adulthood. Proverbs always has its primary relevance to people in this age group.

Proverbs 1:5 is a parenthetical statement that draws attention to a second intended audience for this book—those who are already wise. The sages taught that learning should never stop. There are always new insights to be examined and incorporated into one's life. This admonition does not denigrate the earlier wisdom needed by the young (vv. 2-4). Rather, it encourages those who are more advanced in their understanding—even those who are extremely "wise" (ḥākām) and "discerning" (nābôn)—to remain open continually to new "learning" and "guidance." Lifelong learning is a practice that everyone should embrace. The word for "learning" (leqaḥ) sometimes refers to the influence of persuasive speech (7:21; 16:21, 23). But in the context of 1:5, it indicates understanding derived from good resources, such as the book of Proverbs.

5. Understand Some of the Types of Sayings Sages Used (Prov. 1:6)

The sage mentions four types of essentially synonymous sayings:

(1) A "proverb" (māšāl) is the general term used to describe a variety of types of wisdom sayings (→ "Introductory Sermon," in introduction, p. 19).

(2) The translation "parables" for məlîṣâ is uncertain. The word occurs only one other time in the OT (Hab. 2:6). Scholars attempt to relate it to a better-known root, but no suggestion is universally accepted. Perhaps Fox has the best suggestion; he translates it "epigrams"—"rhetorically polished, artistic sayings or terse poems (as in [Prov.] 6:1-19)" (2000, 64). The NJPS takes this approach.

(3) "The words of the wise" (Prov. 1:6, NRSV; dibrê ḥăkāmîm) could refer generally to all types of wisdom sayings produced by the sages.

Or it could denote those sayings specifically found in written wisdom collections (Longman 2006, 100).

(4) The Hebrew *hîdōtām* is frequently translated "their riddles" (NRSV). But there are no riddles in Proverbs, at least of the type that Samson used in Judges 14:14. Fox suggests that a better translation is "enigmas" (2000, 64-67). Enigmas are sayings that are difficult to interpret because of "ambiguities and obscurities" (65). There are many of these types of sayings in Proverbs.

In summary, the fifth purpose of Proverbs is to guide readers into understanding the sayings that the sages produced and preserved. Specifically, this would include the book itself. Such an endeavor is probably more appropriate for the second audience—those who have already mastered some of the basic principles of wisdom. However, the first audience—the simple and the young—should be challenged to investigate and understand the sayings of the book as well.

Most Importantly, Encourage People to Fear the Lord (Prov. 1:7)

Verse 7 has been called the theme verse for the entire book of Proverbs. It presents the major, underlying theological foundation for the book: gaining wisdom is a religious undertaking. The thesis is this: "All human knowledge comes back to the question about commitment to God" (Rad 1972, 67). Without this commitment, human efforts to gain wisdom will fail. "The search for knowledge can go wrong, not as a result of individual, erroneous judgments or of mistakes creeping in at different points, but because of one single mistake at the beginning" (67). This concept is such a foundational wisdom principle that it is often repeated (Job 28:28; Ps. 111:10; Prov. 2:5; 9:10; 15:33; Isa. 33:6; Mic. 6:9).

The word for "knowledge" (*da'at*) appears sometimes in Proverbs as a synonym for wisdom (see 9:10). It can also refer to the body of information needed to understand the nature of wisdom, as in 1:4. Wisdom has cognitive content as well as a lifestyle. That content includes information about God, the world, and the place of human beings in this world. Knowledge of these is needed for people to become wise. Verse 7 states that the first step in gaining this knowledge is fearing the Lord.

"The fear of the LORD" (*yir'at YHWH*) is the key phrase in this verse. This is not the fear that causes one to break out in a cold sweat when watching a scary movie. Rather, this fear is displayed in the following ways: (1) an overwhelming respect/reverence for God that holds him in awe because of who he is and what he has done; (2) a complete submission of one's life to God that can best be described as that of a servant to the Lord; and (3) a manner of behavior characterized by obedience to God's will, discipline of one's personal life, and worship of God as Lord and Savior. The fact that Cornelius and his household are called "devout and God-fearing" in the NT (Acts 10:2) is an indication that Luke regarded them as living up to the ideal OT standard for wisdom and holy living. The sages also connected the fear of the Lord with turning away from evil. The attraction of our lives toward something good (God) was paired with motion away from something bad (evil) (Prov. 3:7-8; cf. Job 1:1, 8; 2:3; 28:28).

The word "beginning" (Prov. 1:7; *rē'šît*) probably refers both to first in *order* and first in *importance*. The first step in gaining knowledge about life is to reverence God. Take yourself off the podium of your life and put God there. This is not only the first step but also the foundation for everything that follows. It is the foundation upon which to build one's life. There is no more important step that one can take than to set the foundation right. Therefore, it is first in importance as well as in order.

The other side of the coin is that the person who rejects this teaching about life is a fool. Fools (*'ĕwîlîm*) have not taken the first step, which is to build the foundation right, so the superstructure is going to be out of line and wobbly. Fools are people who have no use for God or wisdom (10:23). They live self-centered, sinful lives that refuse all advice (12:15) and "discipline" (1:7; NJPS). For this reason, they are not likely to read the book of Proverbs—a book whose purpose is to teach the ways of wisdom and encourage people to be wise. Fools fill their minds with folly (15:14) and are quick to quarrel with everyone they do not like (20:3). They certainly do not like the sages' advice.

The implication of 1:7 is that wisdom is connected to a relationship with God. One does not become wise simply by going to school, observing human nature, or reflecting on wisdom sayings. The road to wisdom begins by acknowledging the sovereignty of God and submitting one's life to God's direction. People may be quite intelligent and technically skilled, but they are still fools wandering in confusion if they have not submitted their lives to God's sovereignty. The fear of the Lord is the key to understanding this principle.

In this respect, the book of Proverbs says the same thing as the prophets (see Jer. 9:23-24). The only difference is the method of presentation. The prophets get in your face. The proverbs simply state an age-old principle whose observance will lead to a successful life.

What Can We Learn from These Few Verses?

All the reasons why the book of Proverbs was written have to do with wisdom. Wisdom is vitally important to living a good life. Therefore, we need to know the nature of wisdom and how to put it into practice. To become wise, we should seek instructions and disciplined training from others who are already wise. The book of Proverbs, containing hundreds of sayings from wise people in the past, is an excellent teacher and resource for those who are seeking guidance in how to become wise. It should be studied carefully for its insights and applied directly to our thinking and behavior. The young and the naive are especially in need of instruction in wisdom, but everyone can profit by learning more about wisdom from Proverbs.

The starting point for those who are seeking to be wise is learning how to fear the Lord and then actually living in that way every day. People cannot even start to appropriate wisdom into their lives without fearing God. The book of Proverbs is our guidebook on how to do that.

The introduction to the book states that the teachings expressed here have the authority of Solomon—Israel's wisest king—behind them. The book itself contains a number of sayings and instructions that have proven true over centuries of time. Therefore, it should be studied diligently and carefully, and its principles should be lived out daily. There are several areas of application that flow from this main purpose.

1. Being Wise Requires Being Aware of the Big Picture as Well as the Small Details in Life

Most of us spend most of our lives dealing with the small details. These details are important. Paying the bills, getting the kids off to school on time, changing the oil in the car, having one's teeth cleaned twice a year, and shopping for groceries—all have to be done. But there should be a larger picture to life that provides meaning to all of these details. The larger picture is like the background to a painting. The figures in the foreground only have meaning when set against a background that gives context and perspective. People who cannot see the big picture, as the modern proverb puts it, "cannot see the forest for the trees."

Seeing the big picture for the writers of Proverbs entails gaining wisdom through instruction and discipline. This makes Proverbs essential for our spiritual development. It is a valuable teacher that should be read and reread by all. Further, wisdom can only be achieved when we take the first and foundational step of fearing the Lord. Those who refuse to take this first step are fools. The sad consequences of this choice are spelled out in later parts of the book.

2. The Pursuit of Wisdom Requires the Engagement of Both the Mind and the Heart

Proverbs 1:2-6 emphasizes the mental activity of acquiring wisdom, knowledge, understanding, and insight by receiving instruction, guidance, and discipline from other people who are already wise and from the book of Proverbs. Verse 7 stresses the need for the human heart/spirit to reach out to God in fear, reverence, awe, worship, and submission. We must accept God's lordship over our lives. Any attempt to eliminate the mind or the heart from this endeavor or to raise one over the other would be totally rejected by the sages as foolish.

3. Living a Life of Wisdom Affects Our Behavior

The mention of righteousness, justice, and equity in Proverbs 1:3 raises the issue of morality. Sinners and atheists can both gain knowledge of various aspects of life, but only as we choose to fear the Lord can we achieve wisdom about the real nature of life. All genuine wisdom originates with God, and we can only access it when we make the decision to repent of our sins and submit our lives to him.

Such a decision leads to the development of our conscience in ways that influence our behavior. We begin to act and think in ways that agree with God's standard of righteousness, justice, and equity. In this manner, acquiring wisdom brings our behavior into conformity with God's plans and desires for us.

So where are you on the road of life? Have you laid the foundation and taken the first step toward living a life of wisdom? Or are you one our text calls "foolish"—naively wandering through life without God's wisdom to guide you? According to Proverbs, we self-select the category we are in by accepting or refusing God's offer of wisdom.

Possible Sermon Titles: "A Guidebook for Successful Living," "Wisdom or Foolishness: The Choice Is Yours," "A Fork in the Road Leads to Wisdom or Foolishness," "Why Study Proverbs?" "The Purpose of Proverbs," "And God Said, 'Can You Hear Me Now?'" "Setting Goals for One's Life"

II. INSTRUCTIONS (PROV. 1:8–9:18)

The first major section of Proverbs (chs. 1–9) has the form of instructions directed to young people. The intended reader is specifically "my son" (1:8; 3:1, 21; 4:1; etc.). The anonymous teachers are the child's parents—sometimes both parents and sometimes just the father.

This ancient format goes back to the earliest days of proverbial writing in Egypt and Mesopotamia (→ "Introductory Sermon," in introduction, p. 19). This literary device was utilized throughout the ANE. Of course, we all are sons or daughters in need of instructions from our fathers and mothers. We all are learners and students in the school of life. The ancient sages hoped that all readers of these instructions would take their words seriously.

The sermon starters here attempt to comment on each of the major instructions. These are words of wisdom from multiple generations of Hebrew parents to their children. They have been proven true in practical application over hundreds of years.

Peer Pressure (Prov. 1:8–19)

The first topic concerns peer pressure. The word of advice is in essence the following: "Do not fall in with bad companions, who will lead you astray. Rather, listen to the advice of your parents. You may not like their advice, but it is the best advice you can get. Their words have been proven true, and they will enhance your life." Admittedly, there are some exceptions—the small percentage of parents who abdicate their role as good teachers by inflicting neglect, abuse, bullying, and other mistreatments on their children instead of loving them. But in the vast majority of homes, parents strive ceaselessly for the well-being of their children.

Peer pressure is a powerful force all young people experience at some point in their teen years. Suddenly, Mom and Dad's advice on such things as hairdos, clothing, and activities goes unappreciated. Friends at school, at church, in the neighborhood, and online seem to know a lot more about these things than parents. All young people want to fit in and do what their friends are doing. The possibility of yielding to peer pressure only increases after high school. Whether young people are in college or in their own apartments, parents are not around to observe their behavior and offer sound advice. Concerned parents hope their college-age children have learned enough, matured enough, and developed enough self-discipline to resist the most unfortunate appeals of bad companions.

However, our text is about more than what to wear or how to fix your hair. It is about morality. The advice from the sages is, "Do not be led astray by supposed friends who offer you diamonds but give you coal. Choose your friends carefully."

Notice how bad friends are characterized in the biblical text. In Proverbs 1:10, they are called sinners—people who enjoy a lifestyle that opposes God. Verses 11-12 identify them as murderers of innocent people. Verse 13 calls them thieves. Verse 16 identifies them once again as evil murderers. Finally, verses 18-19 describe their attitudes and actions as violent.

The descriptions of these friends are so awful that some interpreters may think the sage must be exaggerating. But twenty-first-century Americans are some of the most violent people on earth in times of "peace." The number of shootings each year is shocking. The number of personal incidents of rage—on the road, in airplanes, and over the internet—continues to rise. In addition, the violent "entertainment" produced by the television, movie, and gaming industries saturates our society. Sadly, we Americans have come to accept violence as normal.

Who would ever want to associate with such bad people? Everything they propose to do is a violation of either community laws or God's law. These things are wrong legally and morally. Yet young people fall into this trap, becoming like the company they keep. Why?

The words of sinners seem to have an enticing, even attractive, appeal. They say, "We have a plan to take other people's things and not get caught. We will get rich. We will have power over other people. We will share everything so that all of us will be better off. We will have our own group, free of parental advice and controls. We can do whatever we want. So, come join us. You'll be a valuable addition to our group." It sounds exciting to defy social norms, to do something bad and get away with it. It is even more alluring to be invited to join a group where people say they care about you and offer to share their benefits with you.

What is the matter with this course of action? Why should young people reject bad companions and listen to their parents? Here is where the sages move beyond just saying, "Do this," or "Don't do that." Wise parents provide good reasons why a certain course of action is beneficial or harmful to their children (Aitken 1986, 17).

The first reason is positive. "A garland to grace your head and a chain to adorn your neck" (Prov. 1:9) are wealthy objects that add visual status and beauty and perhaps even honor to a person's outward appearance. In this passage, they are metaphors for the enhancement to one's character that comes by avoiding association with bad company. A wise son or daughter is attractive in public. The integrity of their character is noticeable and beautiful to all.

The second reason is negative. Bad friends will ruin your life. Their pathway leads to self-destruction (vv. 18-19). So do not take even the first step down that pathway. A later verse in Proverbs adds that God "condemns those who devise wicked schemes" (12:2).

There is great irony here. Those who attempt to destroy others in their pursuit of wealth and good times end up destroying themselves. Their intent on harming others comes back to bite them. The author uses a short proverb here to drive home the point that this is a foolish course of action: "How useless to spread a net where every bird can see it!" (1:17). The proverb has to do with hunting. People who hunt for birds need to set their traps early in the morning and camouflage them before the birds see them. Otherwise, the birds will avoid that area.

This proverb has been interpreted in many different ways. Probably the best interpretation connects verse 17 with verses 18-19. Here the hunters are the bad companions who are spreading their net to capture young people (birds). However, their efforts are useless because the birds can see their intent (at least they *should* see their intent, for young people should be as smart as birds). In the end, the hunters "ambush only themselves" (v. 18). In their rush to capture the birds, they are ensnared in their own net. This interpretation emphasizes the foolishness of sinners who are not perceptive enough to see the destructive end to which they are headed.

Preachers and teachers can draw upon several applications to drive home the point to today's youth. Probably the one that applies most readily is the gang culture that is so prevalent in our inner cities. Gangs offer many positive enticements to lonely teens. It is very difficult for young teens to resist joining a gang when the gang members keep entire neighborhoods in fear. However, the consequences can be tragic. The number of teens who are killed annually in gang-related activities is staggering.

Lest we think that peer pressure applies only to youth, consider the effect on the adult population. Advertising agencies constantly use peer pressure to sell their products. Lobbyists know its value in promoting or attacking proposed legislation.

A good biblical illustration of the tragic consequences of yielding to adult peer pressure is the story of Rehoboam's rise to kingship following the death of his father Solomon (1 Kings 12:1-19). Rehoboam consulted two groups of people about how to answer complaints from the northern tribes. The first group consisted of the wise, older sages and counselors of his father. They told him to respond in a way that showed he cared about the northern tribes. The second group was composed of the young aristocratic friends with whom he had grown up. They encouraged him to act like an authoritarian and order the northern tribes around like slaves. Rehoboam was attracted to the advice of his peers even though they had no experience in governing. Their course of action made him feel powerful. The result was devastating. The northern tribes revolted and left Judah with a smaller territory, economy, and army. The consequences of refusing to listen to the sages could not have been more striking. Rehoboam was forced to rule a small kingdom that was a fraction of the size and power of his father's.

Several years ago, a young, single mom in our community with two kids listened to bad friends who got her hooked on drugs. The police caught up with her and agreed to go easy on her if she would identify her drug dealer. Because of her desire to continue raising her kids, she took their offer and snitched to the police. The drug dealer found out about it and murdered her. When she took her first drug, she probably never considered that it would cost her, her life and that her children would have no parent to raise them. It is a sad story but one that has been repeated hundreds and hundreds of times. People listen to bad friends who lure them to join groups and take up practices that sound very attractive. But the consequences of following that advice are always harmful.

Before finishing this sermon, preachers might offer the young people in their congregations some positive and biblical suggestions for dealing with peer pressure. Can anything else be done in addition to avoiding bad company? Proverbs has two other important directives: (1) get wisdom at all costs, and (2) choose good companions and friends. "Getting wisdom" is probably the most important thing a person can do. The sages plead with young people to do whatever it takes to get it, for it is the key to a successful life (4:1-9, esp. vv. 7-9).

Finding wisdom is not such a hard task, for wisdom's chief spokesperson, "Lady Wisdom," is out in the streets of life recruiting everyone she can find (1:20-21). The more difficult task is applying wise principles of living to every aspect of our lives. This requires self-discipline. Here we need to listen carefully to the sages throughout the book of Proverbs. They do not cover all aspects of human behavior, but they do elucidate many practical areas of life where wisdom can be a tremendous help. Examples of this are practicing good work habits (6:6-11; 10:5; 21:5); having a humble attitude (22:4); loving friends and neighbors (17:17); being generous with the poor (28:27); being kind to enemies (25:21-22); and speaking wisely, honestly, fairly, and calmly (15:1, 4; 16:24; 18:13; 24:26). Not only is wisdom a benefit to the person who accepts it, but it also makes for good relations with everyone around us. It especially makes one's parents happy and proud (10:1; 15:20).

The second admonition is the encouragement: Surround yourself with good friends who will have a positive influence on your life.

Good friends provide love (17:17), loyal support (18:24; 27:10), wise advice (13:20; 27:9), helpful corrections of our opinions (27:17), and a good and righteous environment (2:20). That is exactly what each one of us needs from our friends and companions (→ also the later sermon "Friends and Neighbors," p. 58).

Resisting peer pressure is not always easy, but according to the sages, it must be done if we are to live happy, successful lives.

Possible Sermon Titles: "Gangland Folly," "Gangs Are for the Birds," "How Useless to Spread a Net Where Every Bird Can See It," "Dealing with Peer Pressure," "Peer Pressure Can Destroy You"

Lady Wisdom Is Looking for You (Prov. 1:20-33)

During World War I, the United States government used posters of a fictional character named "Uncle Sam" to recruit young people into the military. The posters pictured a stern, older man pointing his finger at onlookers. The caption read in capital letters, "I WANT YOU FOR U.S. ARMY."

The text in Proverbs 1:20-33 is the recruitment poster of the book of Proverbs. It depicts wisdom personified as a woman (we call her Lady Wisdom). She is out recruiting volunteers in society to accept her words of wisdom and follow her way of life. This reference to Lady Wisdom is repeated in Proverbs 3, 4, 5, 8, and 9. She was a popular topic with the sages.

The sages created her sinister opposite, Lady Foolishness, describing her as adulterous and seductive. She appears in Proverbs 2, 5, 7, and 9. That both characters are female suggests that much of the sages' teachings were directed at young men. In ancient times, boys had a much greater opportunity to receive formal education and training in wisdom than girls did.

The picture of Lady Wisdom in Proverbs 1 is that of an open-air, street preacher walking about the streets of a city warning those who are foolish to "repent" of their sinful ways (v. 23) and "fear the LORD" (v. 29). She takes her message out into the streets, markets, and city gates. She passes near the homes, businesses, and social meeting places of society—anywhere there are foolish people. She is not shy about encountering people. In fact, she searches them out and "raises her voice" (v. 20) so no one will miss her call to change the direction of their lives.

Michael V. Fox suggests that the Hebrew word for "repent" (*šûb*) is not so much a call to repentance as "a call to attention" (2000, 95, 99). "Give heed to my reproof" (NRSV) is Lady Wisdom's challenge for sinners to listen to her and respond to her earlier messages of rebuke. While that may be true, the whole purpose of Lady Wisdom's speech is to get people to change the direction of their lives, to leave their folly and follow her advice. So "repent" probably expresses this thought as well as any translation.

Lady Wisdom's travels about the streets of the city indicate her desire to meet and invite average people on the street. On occasion, she finds herself visiting the palace of the king or the courts of justice (8:15-16). But her primary activity takes place out in society, where ordinary people live and work. This illustrates the sages' belief that wisdom is practical. It belongs in the everyday activities of life.

Wisdom is available to anyone. It is freely offered on every street corner. One does not have to attain a certain level of education, know a secret password, be born into the right family, or have access to someone in a high position. Wisdom is a gift, free for the taking (2:6; Eph. 2:8; James 1:5). Anyone can turn from folly and receive wisdom. Anyone can repent and turn to God.

What is Lady Wisdom's message? She begins with the words "How long . . . ?" (Prov. 1:22). "How long will you continue in your foolish ways and reject the ways of wisdom that will give you a much better life? I am anxiously waiting to share my wisdom with you. I will pour it out in abundance as soon as you indicate your willingness to listen to me. I know my wisdom will change your life. So don't wait another second to respond to my invitation."

There is a sense of urgency about Lady Wisdom's message. Too many people continue to live foolish and sinful lives for far too long.

They need to wake up immediately and stop what they are doing while there is still time to change. Disaster is coming soon. Then it will be too late to respond. The NT echoes this same thought in 1 Thessalonians 5:2-3 and Revelation 3:3.

Lady Wisdom knows it's difficult to get people's attention. She identifies her most challenging audience as the "simple," "mockers," and "fools" (Prov. 1:22). Such people are hard to influence, because they "love" and "delight in" their present lifestyle. They "hate" anyone who challenges them. The next sermon in this book describes each of these persons in detail (→ "Not All Fools Are the Same," p. 46).

Along with her invitation, Lady Wisdom issues a warning to those who reject her advice. "They will eat the fruit of their ways and be filled with the fruit of their schemes" (v. 31; see 14:14). That is, the consequences of their foolishness will not be good. Their mockery of God and their refusal to accept wise counsel will lead to their destruction.

In their time of greatest need, when "disaster" and "calamity" strike them, Lady Wisdom will mock them for their foolishness (1:26-27). They will get no sympathy from her. This may seem rather harsh, for elsewhere Scripture teaches us that God is a God of second chances (e.g., Jon. 3:1; Rev. 2:4-5). Nevertheless, there comes a point when enough is enough. Israel found that out to its regret. Israel spent more than a generation in exile in Babylonia as punishment for breaking the covenant and for failing to repent.

Proverbs 1:28-29 seems to imply that when disaster strikes, mockers may reconsider and turn to Lady Wisdom for help. Why would they call out to her when earlier they rejected her? Is it because they have repented and now want to follow her ways? Or is it because they are desperate and are looking for help to escape from disaster from any possible source? More likely, the latter is the case. There is no indication of any change of heart, for certainly Lady Wisdom would respond to them if they were truly repentant. She knows they will go back to their mocking and foolishness as soon as the disaster is over.

That Lady Wisdom or God would mock or ridicule sinners seems out of character (1:26-27; 3:34). But this concept appears in other places in Scripture (Pss. 2:4; 37:13; 59:8 [9 HB]). Perhaps the best way to understand this image is through the American proverb "The one who laughs last, laughs best." Fools may laugh at Lady Wisdom and think she is old fashioned and totally irrelevant to life today. Still, she will have the last laugh, for someday all fools will learn that they cannot go against the grain of the universe. They will be forced to experience God's judgment for their sinful ways. Then their evil ways will be exposed to God's justice.

The text makes it clear that whatever punishment fools suffer is their own fault. It is not the result of fate. It is not that some are destined to be blessed and some are destined to suffer. It is not that Lady Wisdom's warnings are inaudible to some. No, fools have the same opportunities as wise people, but they have rejected all the advice that Lady Wisdom has to offer. Therefore, they get exactly what they deserve. In one sense, we can feel sorry for them, but in another, we must say, "They chose to live that way. People tried to warn them where they were headed, but they refused to listen. So now they are reaping the consequence of what they sowed" (see Gal. 6:7-10).

Is this much the same situation that exists in today's world? It is true that we use different terminology. We do not talk about Lady Wisdom. We talk about Christ and his offer of salvation. Yet the issue is the same. Are people going to serve God or to mock God and his ways? People have the same opportunity to serve God as they did when these proverbs were written. They hear the same warning about the consequences of turning away from God. The decision to choose between one of two ways is the same today as it was in the days of the sages (see Ps. 1 and Jesus's teachings [Matt. 7:13-14, 24-27]).

The last verse in Proverbs 1 points out the positive rewards that come to those who put aside their folly and turn to God and Lady Wisdom. They "will live in safety and be at ease, without fear of harm" (v. 33). In other words, they will not have to live with the same fear of judgment that the simple, fools, and mockers do. Both internally and externally, they will be at peace (Fox 2000, 103).

This entire passage should put the fear of God in anyone who is living a foolish and sinful life. Lady Wisdom bluntly calls all to repent. Fools and sinners who refuse to listen to her choose to deny themselves of the help God alone can give them when they need it the most (1:28-32; 3:34; 19:29).

The present American Christian culture is reluctant to preach about the consequences of sin and the nature of hell. This is partly due to previous generations' overemphasis on hellfire preaching and attempts to scare people into the kingdom of God. However, the sages suggest that an appropriate fear of God is not a bad idea at all. The sages recognized that different people responded to Lady Wisdom's message in different ways. Her approach probably will not change the mocker's attitude toward God. But it may awaken the simple (19:25; 21:11). They need Lady Wisdom's blunt, confrontational approach.

People have different personalities, so they come to God by different routes. In public education, teachers are trained to adjust their methods of teaching to a variety of students' learning styles. In the same way, preachers need to make room for different religious learning styles in their congregations. The blunt approach of Lady Wisdom will not work with some people.

But "the simple" may listen. They have never entertained a serious thought. They desperately need to hear a full presentation of the eternal consequences of sin to shake them out of their lethargy and point them to a loving God who is ready to receive them with open arms. This point is amply illustrated in the way Jesus used one method to present the gospel to the scribes and Pharisees and another when speaking to tax collectors, prostitutes, and ordinary people—the sheep without a shepherd. Paul echoes this concept in 1 Corinthians 9:19-23.

Possible Sermon Titles: "God's Toughest Audience: The Simple, Mockers, and Fools," "Lady Wisdom Just Walked Down Your Street," "How Long Will You Love Your Simple Ways?" "The Two Ways"

Not All Fools Are the Same (Prov. 1:22)

The focus of the book of Proverbs is wisdom. The book tries to encourage all who read it to make wisdom their number one goal in life. One of the ways it does this is by contrasting those who are wise with the opposite kind of people—fools.

I use the word "fool" here in its broadest sense. Proverbs actually distinguishes between three different types of people who might be called fools—the simple, fools (in a narrower sense), and mockers.

Since Proverbs 1:22 is the only verse in the book to mention all three categories, we use it as our primary text. We will also look at many additional verses as we delve deeply into the dismal world of fools.

Preachers and teachers are well advised to acknowledge Jesus's warning in Matthew 5:22 against calling anyone a fool. Consider what he did and did not mean by this. He probably referred to the second or third type of fool—hopeless, irredeemable reprobates. Recall also that in Luke 12:20, Jesus's parable reports God himself calling a self-obsessed man a fool. The apostle Paul referred to one who boasts as a fool (see 2 Cor. 11:16–12:11). The Bible does not consider all fools the same.

1. The Simple (*pətā'yīm*)

The word that probably best describes the mindset of the simple is the word "naive." The simple lack prudence (Prov. 1:4; 8:5; 19:25), sense (7:7; 9:4, 16), insight (9:6), and wisdom (21:11). *Mentally*, they are unprepared for life because their minds are undisciplined. This leaves them without resources to face temptations, disasters, and complex issues in life. They do not think through the consequences of their choices, and so they make bad and impulsive decisions that are certain to fail (22:3; 27:12). These bad decisions may even lead them to an early death (1:32; 9:16-18).

Simpleminded people live in a fantasy world of "alternative facts" that separates them from reality (12:11). They just drift along through life with no sense of purpose—and they love living this way (1:22). They do not want to change. Their only goal in life is to have fun, so they are easily led astray. They believe anything someone tells them (14:15). Crafty politicians, demagogues, and cult leaders know how to manipulate simpleminded people. More than one American presidential election has been won because of the widespread dissemination of lies and misleading falsehoods. Today's scam artists are experts in knowing how to appeal to the naive and separate them from their money.

The simple are also *morally* unprepared for life (→ later sermon "Lady Foolishness Has Her Eyes on You," p. 65). Proverbs 7:6-27 tells the story of a gullible young man who was seduced by an attractive, older, sinful woman. Her smooth words and appeal to momentary sexual pleasures prompted him to set aside whatever morals he previously had and follow her into her house. The author tells us at the beginning of his story, the young fool "had no sense" (7:7; ḥăsar lēb—lit., he "lacked a heart/mind"). As a result, "all at once he followed her like an ox going to the slaughter" (v. 22a). He was simpleminded and therefore morally unprepared for temptation.

The classification of people as simple is not based on their age or education. Their ignorance is self-chosen. They could be teens or adults who had plenty of opportunities to be educated in the ways of wisdom but rejected all offers. I have known too many first-year college students who displayed the characteristics of the simple. I wanted to say to them, "Get serious about your education. You're wasting a lot of money." Some did get serious by their sophomore year. Others did not return the following year.

One example of a simpleminded teenager in the OT is Joseph (Gen. 37:1-11). He did not have enough sense to keep his grandiose dreams to himself. His naive mindset made his older brothers extremely angry with him and disappointed his father. Moreover, it almost led to his death (v. 20). Joseph eventually matured and recognized the foolishness of his attitude, but it cost him dearly—separation from his family for twenty-two years.

The simpleminded are the people Lady Wisdom and Lady Foolishness seek to change (Prov. 9:4-6, 16). Apparently, hardened fools and mockers are hopelessly mired in their foolish ways. The simple are teachable. The threat of physical harm, to themselves or to others, may wake them up (10:13; 19:25; 21:11). For adults, it could be something like a heart attack, cancer, a serious car accident, or the death of a family member. For young people, it could be failing an exam.

How do the simple become so naive? According to the sages, they inherit their folly from their parents (14:18). While this is not true in all cases, it certainly stresses the importance of good parental teachings and providing examples in the home.

2. Fools (kəsîlîm)

The simpleminded may be naive and wishy-washy, but fools know exactly what they want out of life. They have deliberately chosen to reject God and live a sinful, self-centered life (Prov. 13:19; 14:9;

28:26). As the psalmist notes, "The fool says in his heart, 'There is no God'" (Ps. 14:1). Von Rad calls this "practical atheism" (1972, 65). Fools love doing evil (Prov. 10:23), and they love doing it repeatedly (26:11). They never learn from their mistakes. In sum, they are not right with God, and they never intend to be.

Fools have rejected the wisdom that Lady Wisdom offers and her ordered way of life (1:7; 17:24). They know it is available, for she has invited them to receive it (14:33). However, they have no use for her wisdom or anyone else's (26:7, 9). Neither have they sought knowledge (1:22; 14:7), prudence (8:5), or honor (14:24; 26:1). Their only interest is the immediate gratification of their base desires (10:23; 21:20).

Fools constantly stir up strife with their words (18:6-7; 29:9). Their speech is twisted (19:1). Lies and slander are common (10:18). They get angry easily (12:16; 14:16; 20:3; 29:11). One proverb says they are more dangerous than a mother bear robbed of her cubs (17:12). They will never listen to anyone with a shred of wisdom or ask for help, because they think they know it all (12:15; 14:8; 23:9). They reject all criticism (17:10). They lack knowledge, so their opinions are only folly. However, that does not stop them from blurting out false information (12:23; 18:2). Murphey calls this "verbal diarrhea" (2001, 133). Garbage in, garbage out (15:2, 14).

Another characteristic of fools is their unwillingness to learn from their bad choices and harmful experiences. Like a dog that returns to its vomit, they repeatedly choose disgusting, self-destructive ways and sinful behavior over the life of wisdom God offers (26:11). A further image appears in 2 Peter 2:22—they are like pigs that refuse to stop "wallowing in the mud."

A number of proverbs warn against associating with such fools. They will drag you down and even hurt you (Prov. 13:20; 26:4). You will never learn anything of value from them (14:7; 15:7). You cannot trust them to work for you or carry out an assignment (14:8; 26:6, 10).

The saddest part of the story of fools is the grief they bring to their parents (10:1; 15:5, 20; 17:21, 25; 19:13). They hate their parents and have rejected the godly teachings they received. Their parents are a constant reminder of the moral integrity they lack.

The only way to change such fools is physical coercion. The sages recommended the use of a rod (14:3; 26:3, NRSV). However, beatings do no good, for fools will not change (27:22).

As with the simple, fools are headed for failure in life and an early death. Their attitudes and lifestyle lead to their self-destruction (1:32; 10:8, 10, 14; 14:1; 16:22).

King Saul is a good example of a fool in the OT. In fact, he even admitted that he had acted like a fool (1 Sam. 26:21). His death in defeat by the Philistines and his own face-saving suicide served as God's punishment for his foolish and sinful life.

3. Mockers (*lēṣ/lēṣîm; lāṣôn*—mockery, and *lyṣ*—to mock)

Mockers are at the extreme end of the scale. They are not like the simple—aimlessly wandering through life. They have moved beyond just being fools. They actively ridicule God and his people.

Mockers have an overinflated ego. They think they are right about everything. Everyone else is wrong. Their pride and arrogance prevent them from ever finding wisdom or maturing into intellectual adulthood (Prov. 14:6). Any who attempt to correct them can expect only insults and hatred (9:7-8). They reject the advice of their parents, Lady Wisdom, and God (1:24-25, 29-30; 13:1; 15:12).

Mockers are deliberate troublemakers. They delight in causing strife (1:22; 22:10). Most people recognize the danger of interacting with mockers and seek to avoid them (24:9). Governing officials are aware that mockers have the potential to disrupt entire cities (29:8). Consequently, they construct laws and judicial proceedings to condemn mockers and impose appropriate punishments (19:29). However, the worst consequence for mockers is that imposed by God. His rejection of their mockery will lead to their experiencing suffering, calamity, and destruction (1:26-32; 3:34; 9:12). In the end, God will repay them for their wasted lives of mockery.

The writer of Psalm 1 echoed this thought with these words: "Blessed is the one who does not . . . sit in the company of mockers" (v. 1). If you want to live a blessed life, a meaningful life, a fulfilled life, choose to walk on God's pathway—what Proverbs calls the "way of wisdom" (Prov. 4:11) or the "way of the LORD" (10:29). According to the psalmist, the way of mockers will not survive God's judgment (Ps. 1:5), which leads to destruction (v. 6).

A clear example of a mocker in the OT is Goliath—David's opponent in a battle with the Philistines at the Valley of Elah. Goliath cursed David (1 Sam. 17:43-44) and mocked the armies of Israel (v. 10). He thought his gigantic proportions gave him the power and right to belittle and bully anyone who opposed him. God saw to his defeat by means of the skilled hands of David—a teenage shepherd. Other examples of mockers are the Egyptian pharaoh in the time of Moses (Exod. 5:2) and the Assyrian king Sennacherib in the time of King Hezekiah (2 Kings 18:28-35).

In sum, the main purpose of the sages in speaking of the behaviors and attitudes of the people they called the simple, fools, and mockers was not just to describe and condemn them. It was to warn young people against ever contemplating living such a lifestyle. They recognized that peer pressure (Prov. 1:10-19) has a great influence on young people (as it has in every era and culture). For this reason they wanted to steer Israelite youth away from the pathway of fools.

Today's youth face similar temptations. Perhaps, as you have listened to these words from the sages, God has been speaking to you about some aspects of your own life that are starting to resemble one of these characters—the wishy-washy simple person, or the self-centered fool, or the arrogant mocker. All three make bad moral choices. If you want to change, there is hope for you. God can help you change pathways. God wants to help you change right now before it is too late.

Possible Sermon Titles: "Three Kinds of Fools," "Advice for the Foolish," "Three Blind Mice"

Wisdom's Rewards (Prov. 2:1–3:18)

According to the OT sages, it pays to serve God. It is definitely worth the effort. The entire book of Proverbs promotes the idea that serving God by living a life of wisdom is the best choice a person can make in life. Other ways of living are so much worse.

In Proverbs 2–3, the sages repeatedly remind their "sons" of the value of serving God. They honestly acknowledge that serving God is not always easy. A lifetime of effort is required, and there are many obstacles and temptations to overcome, such as pressure from wicked men and smooth talk from adulterous women. However, the rewards are well worth it. Here are some of the fantastic rewards God offers to those who serve him.

Proverbs in 2:5 refers to the reward of understanding "the fear of the LORD" and finding "the knowledge of God." The two phrases are in parallel and thus similar in meaning. There are also slight differences (→ the earlier sermon "How to Be Successful and Wise," ch. 1, p. 27). "The fear of the LORD" entails acknowledging God's lordship over one's life and living in the light of his lordship. It is a decision made by the heart to submit one's life to God on a continual basis, always holding him in awe and reverence because of who he is and what he has done.

"The knowledge of God" is the recognition of who God is. With that recognition comes a strong desire to fellowship and "bond" (Hartley 2016, 62) with him, to see the world as he sees it, and to promote his agenda. It is a mental activity that seeks to know as much about God as is humanly possible. It is much more than simply accepting certain facts about God. It signifies a commitment to God and his plans for the world.

The fear and knowledge of God are interrelated. The fear of the Lord produces a desire to know more about him. The more one knows about him, the more one recognizes the need to fear him. Both the fear of the Lord and the knowledge of God affect our behavior. They stimulate a desire to live a life that is "right and just and fair" (1:3; 2:9). Moreover, they provide guidance in how to do that.

Therefore, the first reward according to 2:5 is a mature and ever-growing understanding of what it means to fear the Lord and know God. This amazing reward addresses the basic human desire to understand God and his world.

A second reward is described generally in verses 7-8 and illustrated twice in verses 11-19. This reward is protection from wicked/evil people who try to lead the wise away from God. God "guards" and "protects" those who fear him, acting as "a shield" to deflect the enticements of the wicked (vv. 7-8; see Eph. 6:16). Two categories of evil influence are mentioned.

(1) The first is "wicked men" (Prov. 2:12; see vv. 12-15). These people once served God, but now "delight in doing wrong" (v. 14).

They have chosen to live lives of evil and darkness. They pose a danger to those trying to live godly lives because their "perverse" speech and "crooked" behavior can negatively influence people and leave them confused about the truth (vv. 12, 15). As an example of twisted thinking in some parts of our society, all sorts of evil (e.g., violence; sexual improprieties; and prejudices against nations, ethnic groups, genders, and religions) are accepted as legitimate, even though God is displeased with them.

(2) The second wicked person that poses a danger to God's people is the seductive, "adulterous woman"—Lady Foolishness (Prov. 2:16; see vv. 16-19). She has left her first husband and is seeking sexual adventures with someone else. She has a sensuous appeal, but the sages emphasize that those who yield to her smooth talk are headed toward an early death (see 7:26-27; 9:18). Sexual temptations apply to both genders, but the sages were especially concerned with men.

God's protections from these two types of evil do not consist of removing the threat or setting up hedges around us. Rather, God enables his followers to discern the nature of the temptation and to make good choices to reject it (2:11). He gives us a discerning conscience and a spiritual backbone to resist the subtle and not so subtle appeals of the wicked. Jesus prayed that God would do something similar for his disciples (John 17:15).

In Proverbs 3, the sages present nine more rewards for those who serve God. Some of these concern the quantity of life; others, the quality of life (see the commentaries for a further explanation of each):

- Long life, "peace" (well-being), "and prosperity" (v. 2)
- "Favor and a good name" with God and other people (v. 4)
- "Straight" and smooth paths in life—paths that are level, do not zigzag, and don't get lost in the brush (v. 6)
- Good "health" (v. 8)
- "Barns" that are "overflowing" with a good harvest (v. 10)
- "Long life," "riches and honor" (v. 16)
- "Pleasant ways" and "peace" (v. 17)
- A "blessed" life, similar to that in the garden of Eden (v. 18)
- Access to the "tree of life," that is, the source of life (v. 18)

This is a fabulous promotional speech in support of serving God and pursuing wisdom. So why don't more people want to serve God? Shouldn't everyone want to? If a promotional speaker came to your city and advertised a seminar that guaranteed all these benefits above, the auditorium would be packed.

One reason more people do not seek out a life of wisdom is that there are conditions that must be met first. There is a steep cost to gaining wisdom (see the commentaries for a fuller explanation of each):

- You must make wisdom your number one priority in life, seeking it with the same energy that you would seek "hidden treasure" (2:4).
- You must "keep" God's "commands" (3:1).
- You must continually practice "love and faithfulness" (v. 3).
- You must "trust in the LORD with all your heart" instead of relying on your own knowledge and resources (v. 5—one of the most well-known passages in Proverbs; cf. Matt. 6:33).
- You must be humble (Prov. 3:7).
- You must "fear the LORD and shun evil" (v. 7).
- You must give to God the "firstfruits" (i.e., the first and best part) of your income as a thank offering (v. 9).
- You must accept God's "discipline" and correction (vv. 11-12).

Many people avoid a life governed by God and wisdom because they view the effort to meet these conditions as too great. They regard the restrictions on their personal freedom as too severe. In saving themselves, they lose themselves. They fail to recognize the consequences of their foolish choice—consequences outlined in 1:30-33.

Another reason people do not rush after wisdom is because the rewards are generally true, but they are not guaranteed. We all know saintly people who have met all of God's conditions, who are not wealthy or healthy. They have never been recognized as outstanding. And they have died at a young age.

Here is where a proper understanding of the nature of proverbs is essential. Christians need to be honest about this to ward off justifiable criticisms against simplistic claims. The gospel of success (prosperity gospel) cannot explain away the fact that proverbs are not absolute guarantees of success. Here are some ways of looking at

God's rewards that will help better understand how to interpret proverbs like those found in Proverbs 2–3.

1. There Are Consequences to Every Decision in Life

We cannot avoid the cause-and-effect nature of choices and consequences. Sometimes the consequences are delayed, causing questions to arise about God's justice. God may show mercy and fail to send well-deserved judgment, giving sinners another opportunity to repent. However, eventually a life of sin will bring bad consequences, and a life of righteousness will bring good consequences. The writer of Proverbs 2–3 probably overstates his case about good consequences, but he is entirely serious about this matter. He uses all his rhetorical skills to convince people there is only one good way to live, and that is to serve God. He hopes his enthusiastic presentation will cause people to change the direction of their lives.

Jesus mentioned the consequences of choices, trying to convince people to follow him. He noted that the house of the wise stand fast during difficult times, while the house of the fool is destroyed (Matt. 7:24-27). He warned that many people attempt to live an easy life, entering through the wide gate and walking along the broad path. But the end of that path is destruction. On the contrary, few choose the demanding life, with its small gate and narrow walkway. But those who do choose it find real life (vv. 13-14).

Logically, there should be some reward for making right choices in life. Otherwise, why make them? Do you feel you have lived a better life since you became a Christian? You should.

2. Rewards Are Not Always Visible

Sometimes just the internal satisfaction of enjoying a good life is worth far more than money in the bank. God provides both internal and external rewards that are far more valuable than "silver," "gold," and "rubies" (Prov. 3:13-15). In addition, sometimes consequences of our choices are not rewards, but something we avoid. Generally, one can avoid lung cancer by not smoking and sexually transmitted diseases by refraining from sexual relations outside of marriage.

3. The Source of Our Rewards Is Not Always Identifiable

If your house survives a tornado while a neighbor's house is demolished, can that be directly traced to serving God? Probably not. It becomes even more complicated when both you and your neighbor are Christians. Some things just happen in life, and it is useless to try to trace them to moral causes. Their source remains a mystery. Better just to thank God for allowing you to escape an awful tragedy, and then pitch in to help your neighbor recover.

4. Proverbs Should Be Regarded as General Principles That Work on Average, but Not Under All Circumstances

God normally operates according to the principles of wisdom described in the book of Proverbs. If people meet God's conditions and seek out wisdom with all their hearts, then they will likely have much better lives. There are many who can testify that this is true.

However, sometimes other factors enter in—birth defects, accidents, natural disasters, evil people, and growing up in an environment that has few resources and helps. That is exactly the situation in which Job found himself. He was "blameless and upright; he feared God and shunned evil" according to both the author and God (Job 1:1; see v. 8; 2:3). He was the OT's best example of a saint. Yet he still suffered terrible blows to his wealth, his family, and his health. The *other factor* in Job's life was God's test of his faith. He had no idea God would do something like that, so he looked around for some other cause. The sages had taught him that all suffering in life was caused by sin, but Job knew he had not sinned. Therefore, he jumped to the conclusion that God was punishing him unjustly. But he was wrong. God was not punishing him at all.

Here is a lengthy quote from my commentary on Job that should help us interpret proverbs in a more meaningful and realistic way:

> Generally speaking, proverbs are true 99 percent of the time. If they were not, they would never have been preserved and collected into Scripture. The proverbs provide general principles about God's order in the world. They are easily memorized and extremely helpful to parents in teaching the next generation about the proper way to live from God's viewpoint.

However, proverbs are very short and so do not have the space to comment on the circumstances that produce exceptions to the rule. A good example is the well-known proverb: "Pride goes before destruction, a haughty spirit before a fall" (Prov 16:18). Generally speaking, this proverb is true. A self-centered, haughty attitude toward others does lead to one's corruption and downfall. However, everyone knows haughty people who have never experienced destruction, as well as people who have experienced destruction but have never been haughty.

As people move from childhood into adulthood and a more mature understanding of life, they begin to recognize these kinds of exceptions and sometimes begin to question the validity of the original proverb. But there is nothing wrong with the proverb. It still describes the general moral order in God's universe. However, it needs to be balanced with the reality that sometimes there are exceptions that arise due to other factors. And these exceptions create mystery and paradox that cannot be resolved by human investigation, no matter how serious the effort. (Bowes 2018, 412-13)

Therefore, while biblical proverbs are generally true, exceptions do exist because of unusual factors that affect the outcome. Further, God is free to act or not to act as he wishes in governing the world (Prov. 25:2). We may never know the real reason why some days we feel blessed and other days we are suffering. But we can still trust that God knows best about the overall course of our lives and the proper choices that need to be made every day. And we can affirm with the sages that it does pay to serve God and seek wisdom. The sages had it right when they said, "Trust in the LORD with all your heart and lean not on your own understanding; in all your ways submit to him, and he will make your paths straight" (3:5-6). If we will accept that passage as our life's motto, we will have no problem accepting the book of Proverbs as God's faithful and accurate guidebook for successful living.

Possible Sermon Titles: "Does It Pay to Serve God?" "Wise Living and Sinful Living Have Different Consequences," "Wisdom's Rewards"

Friends and Neighbors (Prov. 3:27-30)

Two relationships we all have in life are those with friends and neighbors. These terms are not always equivalents, but in Hebrew both come from the same word—*rēaʿ*. A *rēaʿ* can be a good friend, whether that person lives nearby or far away. Or the term can refer to one who lives next door, but with whom we have no close relationship. The context determines the translation, and sometimes either meaning is appropriate.

Jesus quoted Leviticus 19:18 as the second great commandment (Matt. 22:39): "Love your neighbor [*rēaʿ*] as yourself." Most translations use "neighbor" here instead of "friend" because we already love our friend. The context refers to someone who is more emotionally distant. The command is to treat that person in the same way we would treat ourselves, although that person is not naturally our friend.

In this sermon, we must distinguish between the two translations and deal with them separately, although there is considerable overlap. The sermon begins with the passage in Proverbs 3:27-30. But we will be looking at many other parallel verses scattered throughout the book.

1. Characteristics of a Good Neighbor

In contrast to ancient times when families lived on the same plot of ground for generations, most people today do not choose their neighbors. They find a house or apartment they like and move in, hoping that those living around them will be friendly and respectful. Unfortunately, that is not always the case. One of the questions the sages attempted to address in Proverbs is this: How does one become a good neighbor? Good relationships have to begin somewhere, and the best place to begin is with us.

a. Good Neighbors Fulfill Their Social and Moral Obligations to Others

No matter where one lives—a house, an apartment, or on a farm—there are social and moral obligations between neighbors. Good neighbors act promptly to fulfill these when they are aware of them and have the means to do so (Prov. 3:27-28). Many of them are unwritten, but they are obligations just the same. In biblical times, this meant doing things like returning your neighbor's wandering ox or donkey or helping rescue an animal fallen under the weight of a load (Exod. 23:4-5) (Fox 2000, 165). There also was a moral obligation to tell the truth in a lawsuit involving one's neighbor (v. 2). In contemporary society this admonition could apply to helping a nearby, elderly person with shoveling snow, helping that person get to a doctor's appointment, or helping a nearby farmer harvest his fields while his wife is in the hospital.

b. Good Neighbors Live at Peace with Those Nearby

In Proverbs 3:29-30 the sages cite two instances of unfriendly behavior toward neighbors. The first is plotting to harm them. The second is falsely accusing them of a misdeed. Either one creates an atmosphere of hostility in the neighborhood. The sages encouraged people to be peacemakers in their neighborhoods so that those who know them and live near them will trust them.

c. Good Neighbors Overlook the Shortcomings of Others

All of us have imperfections and idiosyncrasies that can irritate our neighbors. The sages pointed out the value of not speaking about them to the person involved or gossiping about them to others (Prov. 11:12). Give neighbors the benefit of the doubt.

Nevertheless, Proverbs 25:8-10 points out the importance of being straightforward with neighbors. We do not betray their confidences or reveal their faults to others. If we do, they will likely turn on us and broadcast our "dirty laundry" in public. We surely do not want to go to court on an issue and have our neighbors testify against us.

d. Good Neighbors Treat Others with Respect and Kindness

Revenge is a sinful attitude that destroys relationships (Prov. 24:28-29). So is cheating one's neighbor and passing it off as a joke (26:18-19). We should treat our neighbor as we would want to be treated. The Golden Rule (Matt. 7:12) was given for a reason. It encourages people to create an atmosphere in which everyone is treated with dignity and respect (Prov. 14:21). Good neighbors live with that principle in mind. Remember, your neighbors are watching you. You are building a reputation. Build a life of integrity that is centered on God so others will trust you and defend you when you need them. Unkind words and actions have a way of coming back to bite us (13:3).

2. Characteristics of a Good Friend

In contrast to neighbors, friends are people with whom we choose to share our lives and affections. We spend time with them and dialogue with them, both face-to-face and by electronic means. In Proverbs 1, the sages advised avoiding *bad* companions. Scattered throughout the rest of the book are admonitions about choosing *good* companions and being a good friend to them. There is much helpful advice here that all of us need to consider.

a. Good Friends Are There When You Need Them

There are people who cross our paths whom we might call "fair-weather friends" (Kidner 1964, 45). They show up when they see the possibility of receiving some type of benefit—such as when a person comes into great wealth (Prov. 14:20; 19:4). The rich have no problem finding friends. Another example is when someone rises to a position of power and influence (19:6). Kings, presidents, prime ministers, governors, and mayors have multitudes of people around them all the time. The opposite side of the coin is that when people lose their wealth or their position of power, these fair-weather friends are nowhere to be found (14:20; 19:4, 7).

Such so-called friends may temporarily satisfy one's ego. It feels great to be popular or to receive lots of "likes" on Facebook. However, fair-weather friends usually find excuses to absent themselves when you are experiencing trouble. They do not want to be associated with "losers."

A better kind of friend is one who is there when you need them. These people care deeply about your well-being. They are people you would feel comfortable phoning to request prayer for a need.

Relatives and business colleagues are sometimes a source of help when troubles arise, but their interest may be more motivated by obligation than real concern. Such people are exemplified in the three friends who showed up to comfort Job in his time of sickness and sorrow (Job 2:11-13). They are called "friends" by the author because they had known Job in previous years. However, their words throughout the book were anything but friendly. They showed up because they felt an obligation, but they lacked emotional empathy and harassed

Job repeatedly with false accusations. They fit our modern proverb very well: "With friends like these, who needs enemies?"

The sages in Proverbs pointed out that true friends are generous with their love. True friends are people who stick "closer than a brother" (Prov. 18:24) and who love "at all times" (17:17).

Many who read 18:24 are married, but a sizable percentage of the population is single. The primary source of love and fellowship for them is friends rather than spouses. For such persons, this verse provides strong reassurance that good friends can be just as valuable as relatives. In fact, because friends are chosen rather than inherited, they are likely to be even "closer than a brother."

b. Good Friends Are Truthful and Tactful in Their Advice

Knowing what to say to a friend in need of advice is difficult. True friends do not resort to flattery. People who flatter do so (1) to make themselves look good (Ps. 36:2 [3 HB]), (2) to try to get something out of someone (Rom. 16:17-18), (3) to destroy someone (Prov. 29:5), or (4) simply to avoid speaking the truth. Flattery makes people feel good about themselves and about the flatterer. People who flatter know that. But flattery is nothing more than dishonesty and deceitfulness (Prov. 7:21; Ps. 12:2 [3 HB]). Flattery weakens relationships once the flattery is recognized for what it is (Prov. 26:28; 28:23). As Aitken notes, "Beware the kisses of Judas" (1986, 170). The corrections given by a friend are much more valuable than the flattery of an enemy (27:6) because the words of a friend can be trusted to be truthful.

At the other extreme, brutal honesty is seldom the proper approach. Friends do not just blurt out the whole truth, no matter how hurtful, and let the chips fall where they will. Being brutally honest is never wise. People do need to hear the whole painful truth to correct their mistakes. But they need it in the form of constructive criticism from friends who can be trusted (v. 6).

Good friends know that both extremes fail to bring the proper help to someone in need. When giving advice to friends, one needs to be both truthful and tactful. The truth may hurt for a short time (v. 6), but anything less than the truth is a waste of time. A tactful approach that suggests ways to improve the situation, while honestly identifying the problem, gets the best results.

c. Good Friends Know the Value of Dialogue

Proverbs 27:17 makes a remarkable comparison: "As iron sharpens iron, so one person sharpens another." This sounds like an invitation to conflict, but it actually acknowledges that we need each other to sharpen our thinking skills and gain sound wisdom. "One cannot become wise by oneself" (Clifford 1999, 239). Through dialogue, friends can act as safe sounding boards for ideas and opinions still in progress. We will not always see eye to eye with our friends. Personalities are different, so we should expect there to be differences of opinion. Good friends know how to talk through their differences and how to disagree agreeably. They have discovered that a healthy dialogue between different personalities strengthens and sharpens both parties.

d. Good Friends Love You No Matter What

There are times in our lives when we are simply unlikable. Stress, illness, emotional pain, overwork, reverses in life, and other matters may make us grumpy and unpleasant to be around. However, according to the sages, "A friend loves at all times, and a brother is born for a time of adversity" (Prov. 17:17). The constant love of a friend is an invaluable gift. The appearance of such a friend at a time of great difficulty in our life is like applying perfume to a stinky situation (27:9). It completely changes and freshens up the atmosphere.

3. Good Friendships Must Be Nurtured to Thrive

Clearly, good friends are wonderful blessings, who provide all kinds of benefits. Good neighbors are valuable too. That being so, good relationships with other people are vulnerable. They can be destroyed if not nourished and protected. Two students can be the best of friends. At the next exam, one of them gets an A despite spending little time studying, while the other gets a D after staying up all night. The next day they are not talking to each other. Two girls can be the best of friends until one of them gets a date to the Valentine's Day party and the other does not. Suddenly jealousy rears its ugly head causing the breakup of a once happy relationship.

In Proverbs, the sages share several practical ideas that can help to protect our friendships and neighborly relationships.

a. Don't Talk about Friends behind Their Backs

Nothing destroys a friendship quicker than gossiping about people (Prov. 16:28). Good relationships are built on trust. Once trust is destroyed, friendships struggle to survive.

b. After Tactfully Counseling a Friend in a Constructive Way, Let the Matter Lie

We all know we have many faults that need correction, and good friends are helpful in counseling us about how we can make effective changes. Yet no one likes to hear their faults exposed repeatedly (Prov. 17:9). Once is enough. Further discussion of the matter should be avoided, or it may appear to be demeaning.

c. Don't Take Advantage of a Friend's/Neighbor's Time

Friends provide great support and benefits to a person's life, but too much of a good thing will spoil the relationship (Prov. 25:17). Give your friends some space. They do not want you in their face all the time. They have other friends they like to be with too.

Another unkind behavior appears in 27:14. Praising one's neighbor is certainly a respectful gesture, but praise in a loud voice, early in the morning, is not a good thing. A good neighbor seeks to do the right thing at the right time.

d. Avoid Making Friends with People Who Get Angry Easily

A friendship cannot be sustained with those who are angry all the time (Prov. 22:24-25). The immediate danger to you is that their traits will rub off on you. You will get angry whenever they do. But eventually they will get angry at you, too, and leave. In addition, no one likes to be around angry people, so your association with such individuals will drive good friends away from you.

e. Don't Loan Money to Friends and Neighbors

Because love is a key ingredient in any friendship, the natural inclination is to loan money to a friend in need or sign a guarantee that you will make good a friend's loan. The sages had witnessed too many such relationships go sour over business deals (Prov. 6:1-5). The reason is that a loan or guarantee places two people in a business relationship. Our judgment and expectations in business will likely be clouded by our friendship. When the arrangement goes bad, it will probably lead to the dissolution of the friendship. So the sages' advice is to avoid loaning money and signing guarantees for friends (17:18; 22:26-27). A better approach is simply to give friends the money they need. Then no expectations will ever be dashed. A good illustration of a business arrangement that could easily go sour is hiring a friend to build your new house.

The principles outlined in the sermon above were proven true by generations of sages. They describe the kinds of friends or neighbors we would dearly love to have. They are a positive counterweight to the description of bad companions in Proverbs 1. Most parents want their children to choose friends carefully, exactly like the model held up by the sages: "The righteous choose their friends carefully" (12:26a; the translation of this verse is uncertain; my interpretation follows the NIV).

However, the process of finding good friends and neighbors begins with us. People need to *be* good friends to *find* good friends. Those who feel they lack good friends should probably do a personal inventory of their own friendship skills. That may require the wise counsel of a trusted friend or relative, since we are often reluctant to admit our own failures. Once weak spots have been identified, the process of improvement can begin.

Before concluding this sermon on friends and neighbors, let us look at one more topic. We have looked at some good principles to guide our relationships with other people. What is the status of your friendship with God? Jesus made this powerful statement on the night before his crucifixion: "Greater love has no one than this: to lay down one's life for one's friends. You are my friends if you do what I command. I no longer call you servants, because a servant does not know his master's business. Instead, I have called you friends, for everything that I learned from my Father I have made known to you" (John 15:13-15).

Several things are indicated in this passage. (1) Jesus wants to be our friend. (2) Jesus has provided the means to start a friendship with us by laying down his life. (3) Jesus offers his friendship to all who humble themselves and ask for his forgiveness. Finally, (4) Jesus offers his friends the knowledge and wisdom he has received from his Father concerning how to live a successful life.

Jesus's offer of friendship sounds very attractive and convincing. He has started the game of life and placed the ball in our court. The question he wants us to answer is, How badly do you want to be his friend? Again, the book of Proverbs is our guide. Friendships must be nurtured on both sides. God has done his part. Are you ready to do your part? "Trust in the LORD with all your heart and lean not on your own understanding; in all your ways submit to him, and he will make your paths straight" (Prov. 3:5-6).

Possible Sermon Titles: "Good Friends and Neighbors," "When Iron Sharpens Iron," "With Friends like These . . ."

Lady Foolishness Has Her Eyes on You (Prov. 7:1–27)

There are four lengthy passages in the instructions section of Proverbs that deal with "Lady Foolishness"—the adulterous, seductive, evil counterpart of Lady Wisdom (5:1-23; 6:20-35; 7:1-27; 9:1-6, 13-18). Each is framed somewhat differently. Chapters 5 and 6 simply warn young men, "Do not get involved with Lady Foolishness. She will destroy your life." Chapter 7 is a parable about the adventures of a young man who falls for the smooth talk of Lady Foolishness. In chapter 9, Lady Wisdom and Lady Foolishness compete for the attention of young men. Their houses sit on opposite sides of the street. Each calls out to the young men who pass by, inviting them to a banquet at her house.

Of course, both leading ladies are merely personifications of divine wisdom and earthly folly. God is the source of all wisdom. He freely offers this guidance: Wisdom comes through obedience. We learn to recognize the truth by submitting to God's instruction. It is folly to live in any other way. The temptation to rebel against God arises from the illusion that unrestrained independence is possible. Those who surrender to their baser instincts fool themselves. Their imagined freedom is actually a life of perpetual slavery and eventual self-destruction. The narrative is a memorable moral lesson about the inevitable consequences of personal choices.

This sermon focuses on the attractive storyline of chapter 7. Of course, preachers and teachers can use any of the four passages as their primary text and supplement it with comments from the other three.

As already noted, the literary form of chapter 7 is a parable. It tells the story of the downfall of a young man whose life is ruined by yielding to sexual temptation. The story begins with the father's advice to his son to avoid the woman he is about to describe. He advises his son instead to pay attention to "wisdom" (v. 4).

The imaginary man in the story is described in verse 7 with three characteristics: First, he is "young." Second, he is "simple" (i.e., naive about the dangers in life). Third, he has "no sense" (that is, he lacks the ability to make good decisions). In other words, he is totally unprepared for the nighttime encounter he is about to have with Lady Foolishness. He is the sort of person who needs all the advice he can get from Lady Wisdom. Unfortunately, he carelessly ignores her.

Lady Foolishness, on the other hand, is well prepared for the evening's activities; she has done this many times before. She is older and more experienced than the young man. She knows how to get the attention of young men; she is "dressed like a prostitute" (v. 10). During the day she is "crafty," loud, and self-confident (vv. 10-11). But at night, she probably speaks in hushed tones to avoid detection. Her words "drip" with the sweetness of "honey" and the smoothness of "oil" (5:3). She prowls around the streets of the city looking for naive young men. There is no way to avoid meeting her, for she is everywhere ("at every corner she lurks" [7:12]). Temptation is inevitable, but God has provided "a way out" (1 Cor. 10:13).

The sage who told this story was obviously directing his fatherly comments to young men—as a father would speak to his son (Prov. 7:1). The fictional lady is the temptress, the wicked person, bent on leading the naive astray. Obviously, the genders could be reversed, which is probably more common today than the situation in Proverbs. In today's world, fathers and mothers might warn their daughters of evil men on the prowl. Preachers speaking to a congregation of both men and women should make this clear. The account of David's affair with Bathsheba demonstrates that men may instigate adultery as well as women (2 Sam. 11:2-4; see Job 24:15, which refers to a male "adulterer").

Sexual temptation is not unique to the modern or ancient world. Chances are that some in your congregation have had to deal with it as recently as last week. Therefore, they may easily identify with the characters in this story. This young man wandered into a trap, where he was forced to do battle with the forces of evil. It was an unequal battle, because he was unprepared. He was too naive to listen to the advice of Lady Wisdom.

The sage described the tactics the seductive woman used to break down the self-control of the young man, if he ever had any. First, she gave him the "shock treatment," a big smack on the lips (Prov. 7:13; Kidner 1964, 75). That would get anyone's attention. The forwardness of an unexpected kiss would have been even more so in ancient times. This woman clearly communicated that she liked him. This was his special day.

Second, the woman claimed she had just made a "fellowship offering" at the temple to fulfill a religious vow (v. 14). (She was a religious woman!) She had plenty of meat left over to share with someone. This young man was the fortunate one she had chosen (vv. 14-15).

Third, she appealed to the boy's senses by describing her bedroom. Her bed was extravagantly decorated with "colored linens from Egypt" and perfumed with expensive "myrrh, aloes and cinnamon" (vv. 16-17). The impression she wanted to make was that she was rich and exciting.

Finally, she offered the young man an invitation: "Come to my house and let's make love tonight" (v. 18, author's paraphrase). Lest he be wary of her husband coming home and finding them together, she reassured him that her husband had gone on a long trip (vv. 19-20). He would not be back for weeks, so nothing would interrupt them. No one would ever know what they'd share together. The opportunity was perfect for love.

Lady Foolishness was obviously a woman on the prowl. Like a lioness in the bush, she had spotted her prey and was now circling for the kill. How would the young man escape this appealing, sensuous, seductive encounter?

According to the sage, he would not, for he had not prepared himself in advance by listening to Lady Wisdom. He was now under the sway of this adulterous woman. She had gained his full attention by her physical appearance, her offer of fine food and sexual thrills, and her smooth, seductive speech.

"All at once he followed her" is the sage's graphic description of this young man's surrender to the temptress (v. 22). He headed off into the night with his "lover." The sage emphasized the stupidity and tragedy of his decision with three similes: "like an ox going to the slaughter," "like a deer stepping into a noose," "like a bird darting into a snare" (vv. 22-23). He had no chance of survival. His doom was inevitable.

The sage concluded the passage by repeating the moral advice given at the beginning. Stay away from Lady Foolishness (vv. 24-27). She has destroyed many young men before you. Her home is the entrance to Sheol—the place of the dead. You will never escape her house once you enter.

At this point, preachers and teachers need to decide how to apply the story to a local congregation. There arc several possibilities:

One is to focus on the sin of adultery using 5:1-23 and 6:20-35 as background material. There are several warnings in these chapters about the pitfalls that await adulterers. This is a neglected topic in many churches today. Even many churchgoers are guided more by situation ethics than by the Bible.

A second possibility is to emphasize the choice the young man must make between the two women in 9:1-6, 13-18—Lady Wisdom or Lady Foolishness. Their attitudes, lifestyles, and destinies are much different. Like the young man, we all must make serious decisions. Our choices will determine our success or failure, and our eternal destiny. Will we choose wisely or foolishly? The sages sought to help people make good choices. This emphasis on the two ways in life appears also in Psalm 1, Deuteronomy 31:15-20, and in Jesus's teachings (e.g., Matt. 7:13-14, 24-27; 25:1-13).

A third possibility, which I have chosen, focuses on the topic of temptation. Here are several lessons we can learn from Proverbs 7.

1. Temptation Is All around Us

The story in Proverbs 7 refers explicitly to sexual temptation, but temptation is much broader than that. Lady Foolishness is on every street corner—Wall Street and Main Street as well as in the red-light district. In today's world, people do not even have to go outside their houses to run into her. She is all over the internet. Jesus had three temptations just after his baptism (Matt. 4:1-11). None of them had to do with sex. They appealed to his desire for power, fame, and control.

Lady Foolishness even comes to church. In the story, she mentioned paying a vow that day. That remark was intended to deceive the young man into thinking she was religious. (See Hartley's insightful comments about the dangers of Christian men and women letting their guard down; 2016, 101-2.) One can mistakenly assume that the other person is too spiritual to initiate an illicit affair. Good people who let Lady Foolishness lead them down the sensuous path have destroyed more than one Christian marriage.

Religious solicitation can manifest itself instead as ill-advised business arrangements that end in financial disaster. Even poor preachers have fallen victim to get-rich-quick schemes. Some economic decisions that are not dishonest are clearly unwise. Millions of Americans are drowning in credit card debt, fueled by our consumer culture and the subtle temptation to acquire possessions—new houses, furniture, appliances, cars, boats, recreational vehicles, and the list goes on.

Or imagine two Christians sharing a meal at a restaurant. One encourages the other to join him in a "nice drink." It does not have much alcohol. Besides, how could anything that tastes so good be bad for you? Who knows? Could this innocent sip be the entry into a life of alcohol addiction?

If we deny that temptation is around us wherever we are, we are only kidding ourselves. We are setting ourselves up for a fall. Better to be warned and prepared with our battle armor on (Eph. 6:10-17) than to assume naively that we will never yield to temptation.

2. Temptation Is Often Subtle, So We Must Always Be on Guard

The young man in the story was clearly putting himself at risk by wandering down Lady Foolishness's street at dusk. This was her street. He was entering her territory. The time of day would conceal whatever he did from observation by others. It was dinnertime, so he was hungry. He was simple—he was so naive that he believed no one would bother him. The advantage was clearly in her favor, because he was unprepared.

The tricky part about temptation is that sometimes its appeal is confused with legitimate opportunities. In Proverbs 9:1-6, 13-18, Lady Wisdom and Lady Foolishness both had houses on opposite sides of the street. They made identical pitches to the people walking by: "Let all who are simple come to my house!" (9:4, 16). Sometimes evil sounds so good that it almost sounds like the truth. Often its appeal is enhanced with neon lights and graphic images. Natural desires for food, shelter, companionship, fun, health, and wealth can be twisted into wicked ways to achieve them. So one must always be on guard against the subtle tricks of Lady Foolishness.

3. The Consequences of Yielding to Temptation Are Always Negative, to Those Directly Involved and to Their Families

Two proverbs drive that point home. If people play with "fire," they will be "burned." If they "walk on hot coals," their "feet" will be "scorched" (Prov. 6:27-28). The sages noted the following consequences with regard to adultery: physical "blows," "disgrace," and "shame" in their community, in addition to having to face the "fury" of the adulteress's husband (vv. 33-35), "who will have the support of the law behind him as he seeks revenge" (Longman 2006, 176).

Joseph experienced Potiphar's fury even though he was completely innocent of seducing Potiphar's wife (Gen. 39:19-20). Today, adultery may not result in physical blows, but "it still leads to alimony, child support, broken homes, hurt, jealousy, lonely people, and venereal disease" (Waltke 2004, 313).

The final consequence of yielding to temptation is "death" (Prov. 5:5, 23; 7:27; 9:18). Certainly, spiritual death occurs, but an early physical death could also result due to the husband's fury. The young man's marriage would also be in danger, since his wife would not be pleased to learn about his affair. As the apostle Paul recognized, "The wages of sin is death" (Rom. 6:23).

In the story, the young man thought he could get away with his illicit liaison with Lady Foolishness. It was night, the woman's husband was gone, and no one would ever know. The typical mindset of the sinner is, "I will never get caught." However, Proverbs 5:21 notes that there is one from whom we can never hide: "For your ways are in full view of the LORD, and he examines all your paths." Every reader knows the outcome of the story in advance. Unfortunate consequences for adultery are guaranteed.

4. Self-discipline Is Needed to Overcome Temptation

The sages stressed the importance of "discipline" as a means of triumphing over temptation. Parents and teachers need to begin instilling principles of wisdom early in the lives of their children/students. Time is needed to develop good habits of mental preparedness for when Lady Foolishness will come along (5:1-2, 11-14; 6:20-24; 7:1-5). Without discipline, a person's life will end early (5:23). Everyone must practice self-discipline to avoid contact with Lady Foolishness. She has already destroyed the lives of many others (7:26-27); stay away from her! Do not even walk by her house out of curiosity (5:8).

Instead, Proverbs urges young people to direct their love and sexual desires toward their own spouses (5:15-20). "May you ever be intoxicated with her love" (v. 19). This is how the sages summed up the goal of the young man's affection. A good marriage was to be a strong deterrent against the temptations of Lady Foolishness. If people are mentally, emotionally, and sexually committed to their own spouses, the temptations of the adulterous woman will never find an opening. Goldingay notes, "By all means be crazy for love, Proverbs urges, but make sure it's your wife you're crazy for, otherwise you'll end up being simply crazy and paying the penalty for it" (2014, 26).

The sages emphasized the importance of mental discipline to keep one's thoughts in the right place. "Lust" is the first step toward adultery (6:25). Jesus noted that it is such a threat to right living that losing an eye would be preferable to the consequences of lust (Matt. 5:27-30). Today, the sages would probably have strong words of warning against pornography in all of its manifestations. They would agree with Martin Luther, who reportedly said, "You can't keep the birds from flying over your head, but you can keep them from making a nest in your hair."

5. Ask God for Help with Temptation

In Proverbs 7:1-5, the sage appeals to his student/son to listen to Lady Wisdom and follow her advice: "Respect her as if she were your older 'sister' or an older friend who knows way more about life than you do" (v. 4, author's paraphrase). Establishing a familial relationship with Lady Wisdom provides not only a loving relationship but also valuable advice concerning the tactics of Lady Foolishness.

The intent of this admonition is to focus on what worked in the past. The sages did not appeal to the law, or in this case to the seventh commandment (Exod. 20:14), for direction about how to live. They appealed to the wisdom of the ages that had been proven true over and over again. They had observed that sexual affairs never produced good results.

As we saw in Proverbs 1, Lady Wisdom is out in the public areas of life seeking to rescue every single person from a life of folly and sin. Her call is loud and persistent: "Repent" (v. 23), she says. "Come follow me and I will reward you in many significant ways" (author's paraphrase; → earlier sermon "Wisdom's Rewards," p. 51). Her advice is like a "lamp" on the pathway of life. It "will guide you," it "will watch over you," and it "will speak to you" about how to live a successful life, providing "correction and instruction" when needed (6:22-23).

In the NT, Paul echoed Lady Wisdom's words by urging the church at Corinth to take the matter of temptation seriously (1 Cor. 10:12-13): "Do not be overconfident that you can defeat it by yourself. You need God's faithful help to recognize it, to endure it, and to escape from it. And he will do all three if you trust him" (author's paraphrase). So ask him for help. "Trust in him at all times, you people; pour out your hearts to him, for God is our refuge" (Ps. 62:8 [9 HB]).

Possible Sermon Titles: "The Temptations of Lady Foolishness," "Dealing with Sexual Temptation," "Young Man! Watch Where You're Going!"

Lady Wisdom's Remarkable Character and Usefulness (Prov. 8)

This chapter was a key passage in Christological debates during the fourth century AD. The limited scope of this book does not allow me to address these issues and arguments. Suffice it to say that the formulation of the Nicene Creed was influenced by the controversy (see commentaries and historical theologies for more explanation).

Several passages in Proverbs personify wisdom as a woman. Chapter 8, the longest passage, is actually one long poem. It is beautifully constructed with a short introduction by the author (vv. 1-3) and a long speech from Lady Wisdom, divided into four sections (vv. 4-36).

This chapter contains the OT's most serious reflection on Lady Wisdom's relationship with God. NT writers used it to draw parallels between Wisdom and Christ. We examine the main topics in this chapter, look briefly at its influence on the NT, and comment on its relevance today. Preachers might do well to use this passage during Advent.

The introduction (vv. 1-3) begins with imagery already familiar from earlier chapters. Lady Wisdom was out on the streets of the city pleading her case. She traveled the roads and visited the gate of the city where people pass by and congregate. She called out to everyone in hearing distance.

In the first section, Lady Wisdom fervently pled with everyone to listen and to choose her way of life. Her words grab our attention (vv. 4-11): "Please stop what you are doing and listen to me! Heed my trustworthy words of wisdom. Leave your life of foolishness. Follow my advice, and you will gain something far more valuable than silver or gold. You will gain wisdom about how to live, for my mouth speaks only the truth. If you listen to me, you will know what is right and just to do" (author's paraphrase).

Lady Wisdom's message was for every human being, but she was especially interested in finding people who lacked good sense—simpleminded folks and the "foolish" (v. 5). She wanted to wake them up, to make them aware of the dangers of the foolish path they were traveling. She wanted to call them to a much better life—the way of wisdom. They would never regret accepting Lady Wisdom's guidance and walking her pathway, for "nothing you desire can compare with her" (v. 11).

In the second section of her speech (vv. 12-21), Lady Wisdom identified four things she hated—"pride," "arrogance," "evil behavior," and "perverse speech" (v. 13). She hated them because they were evil—the antithesis of godliness. They manifested themselves in self-seeking and self-promotion. Instead, people needed to acknowledge the preeminence of God in their lives. Lady Wisdom cannot tolerate any attitudes or actions that lead people away from God.

Lady Wisdom continued to describe her influence on community leaders (vv. 14-16). They needed her counsel and insight to make good decisions and govern wisely. She also mentioned the importance of righteousness and justice to her. She would bestow riches and honor on those who follow her ways (vv. 18-21).

In the third section (vv. 22-31), Lady Wisdom told of her relationship to God and her continued usefulness to him. He brought her into being at the very beginning of time. In fact, she was the first thing he created. Before the earth and the heavens existed, before the mountains and the seas, before the appearance of humanity, God gave birth to Lady Wisdom. She remained at God's side, helping him and rejoicing with him in what he was bringing forth in the physical world (compare the rejoicing of the divine beings when God created the world in Job 38:7). She was especially delighted when he created human beings (Prov. 8:31). Fritsch calls verse 22 "the highest conception of wisdom found in the canonical books" (1955, 4:830).

The exact meaning of verse 30 is unclear due to disagreements over the translation of the Hebrew 'āmôn. The NIV has "constantly," the NRSV "like a master worker," and the NJPS "as a confidant." Fox suggests "growing up" (2000, 264). Each provides a different plausible nuance (see the commentaries). Regardless, the verse clearly implies that Lady Wisdom remained at God's side the entire time, assisting him while he crafted the world into existence. She was tremendously useful to him.

In the fourth section of the poem (vv. 32-36), Lady Wisdom exhorted everyone to accept her message and follow her ways. If they did, they would "find life and receive favor from the LORD" (v. 35). But if they rejected her, they would receive harm and death. This promise of a blessing and warning of a curse reflects other OT passages (e.g., Deut. 30:11-20; Ps. 1).

Proverbs 8:22-31 is an extraordinarily significant passage because of its influence on later writings. Two of them are preserved in Jewish literary works found in the Apocrypha.

In Ecclesiasticus (ca. 180 BC), the author, Jesus son of Sirach, noted that God created Wisdom and then "he poured her out upon all his works, upon all the living according to his gift; he lavished her upon those who love him" (Sir. 1:9-10, NRSV). In a later passage, Lady Wisdom spoke of her relationship to God: "Before the ages, in the beginning, [God] created me, and for all the ages I shall not cease to be" (24:9, NRSV). In the same chapter she described how God appointed her to reside in Israel (vv. 8-12) and how she came to be associated with the Torah, the law of Moses (v. 23). The OT had already hinted at this connection in Psalms 19:7 [8 HB] and 119:72, 98.

In the second book of the Apocrypha, the Wisdom of Solomon (late first century BC or early first century AD), the author described Lady Wisdom's participation with God in creation. He called her "the fashioner of all things" (Wis. 7:22; also 8:6, NRSV). He described her as "an initiate in the knowledge of God, and an associate in his works" (8:4, NRSV). Other passages assign her an even higher status: "For she is a breath of the power of God, and a pure emanation of the glory of the Almighty. . . . For she is a reflection of eternal light, a spotless mirror of the working of God, and an image of his goodness" (7:25-26, NRSV).

In the NT, Proverbs 8 also influenced the writers of the Gospels and the Epistles. Luke mentions that Jesus "was filled with wisdom" (Luke 2:40) and he "grew in wisdom" (v. 52) during his formative years. At the beginning of Jesus's teaching ministry in various towns in Galilee, people often expressed amazement at what he said (4:32, 36). He spoke with an authority unlike their rabbis and scribes. When Jesus returned to his hometown of Nazareth, the people who had known him as a child were amazed at his teachings and wisdom (Mark 6:2). Matthew 11:18-19 reports that Jesus made a direct connection between Lady Wisdom and himself; she was proved right by her actions, and so was he. In Matthew 11:28-30, Jesus invited people to come to him for rest and refreshment, just as Lady Wisdom had in Proverbs 9:5-6. Later in his ministry, Jesus even claimed that his wisdom surpassed that of Solomon (Luke 11:31).

In the Epistles, the connection between Wisdom and Jesus is much more theological in nature, focusing on Christ's role in creation. In 1 Corinthians 1:24, 30, Paul called Christ "wisdom from God," that is, God's wisdom in human form. In Colossians 1:15-20, he called Christ "the firstborn over all creation" (v. 15). Christ's connection with the rest of creation was this: "All things have been created through him and for him" (v. 16). Colossians 2:2-3 called Christ "the mystery of God . . . in whom are hidden all the treasures of wisdom and knowledge." In Hebrews 1:2, God appointed his Son "heir of all things, and through whom also he made the universe."

But the most significant passage that connects Christ with Lady Wisdom is the prologue to John's Gospel (John 1:1-14). There in verse 1, Christ, as the *Logos*/Word, was not only with God, as was Lady Wisdom, he was also God himself. As God, he was there in the beginning (v. 1), and through him, all creation came into being (v. 3). Such language takes us well beyond Lady Wisdom's connection to God in Proverbs 8. Much more could be said about this topic (for Wisdom's relation to *Logos*, see Tobin 1992, 4:348-56). Clearly, the NT used the OT's descriptions of Lady Wisdom to reflect on the identity of Christ and expand them even further.

What, then, does this significant chapter say to us today? Here are four ways that Lady Wisdom is still invaluable to humanity.

1. Wisdom Calls to Every Human Being

In the introduction, Lady Wisdom is out in the streets of life doing everything she can to reach everyone. She claims to have an ordered plan for each of our lives, including wise and truthful answers to all of life's issues and problems. She does not want to keep them to herself. She is a people person who wants to meet all of us and share her insights. Accordingly, she makes her way throughout the city of life, trying to engage everyone she sees in conversation.

Lady Wisdom knows that we all live busy lives. She is aware that many people and things compete for our interests and time—family, jobs, friends, church activities, shopping, hobbies, sports, and entertainments. But she also knows we need her to be successful in life. Without her ordering principles, our lives will be disorganized and meaningless. Thus she goes everywhere there are people and calls out loudly to gain our attention (Prov. 8:1). Right now, she is calling out to each of us.

2. Each of Us Needs Wisdom's Offer

Lady Wisdom makes an astounding statement in Proverbs 8:11: "Nothing you desire can compare with her." Think for a moment about all the things that people desire in the world. There is a multitude of them. There are necessities such as food, clothing, and shelter. Others want a job or a loan. Still others are looking for companionship or marriage and children. Some are lonely and need a friend. A few are seeking great wealth and luxuries. On the TV program *Who*

Wants to Be a Millionaire? the host used to ask the contestants after they had won about $32,000, "What are you going to do with all that money?" One frequent answer was, "Pay off all my bills." What do you think their bills looked like a year later? The more people get, the more they want.

In the weeks leading up to Christmas, the advertising industry tries to speak to people's desires. Since Christmas is a season of giving gifts, advertisers try to influence us to buy their products. "You've just got to buy these tools for your husband." "Your wife really needs this jewelry." The ads imply that these gifts will meet your needs, bring happiness, and improve your relationships. The advertisers also try to influence us to buy gifts for our pets. There are now even Christmas lights to put on our dogs or in our fish tanks!

Lady Wisdom tells us that nothing we desire—whether at Christmastime or just in general—can compare with her wisdom. That is an amazing statement. Whether you own a million-dollar house or are homeless, whether you are in great health or dying of terminal cancer, whether you are retired or working two jobs, it does not matter. Lady Wisdom is coming to you and making a priceless offer—wisdom. It is worth more than anything else you could desire in this world. It is worth more than any present under your Christmas tree.

Sometimes we find ourselves in situations that seem impossible and overwhelming. Mountains rise up on every side. There seems to be no way forward. Lady Wisdom's answer is, "Give your problems to me. 'I was there' [v. 27] from the beginning of creation. I know God's mind. I know his heart. I know he has an answer for whatever your problem is, and I will help you find it."

3. Wisdom's Benefits Are Life Changing

In Proverbs 8:14-21 Lady Wisdom speaks of the many benefits she can provide for those who seek her and follow her ways. Some are material benefits, such as "riches and honor" (v. 18; see v. 21). Some are intellectual benefits, such as "knowledge, insight, sound judgment, prudence, discretion, shrewdness, and strategic planning (2:2, 6, 7, 10-11; 3:21; 5:2; 8:12, 14)" (Hartley 2016, 109). Some are societal benefits, such as good government and wise decrees (8:14-16). Some are moral assets, such as "righteousness" and "justice" (v. 20).

The most significant gift she offers is love for everyone who seeks her (v. 17). She is already seeking us and inviting us to follow her ways. If we choose to do so, we will receive not only the benefits of her knowledge about life but also the warmth of her love and care for us. That in turn prompts our love for her, what Fox calls "an emotional commitment" (2000, 275).

The gift of being loved and loving in return is life changing and certainly far more valuable than the finest silver and gold (vv. 10-11, 19). It is like being born again into a new life with new insights, new goals, new relationships, and new hope. How can we not love this Lady who can refashion our lives into ones that are ordered, successful, and pleasing to God?

4. Wisdom's Characteristics and Activities Point Us to Christ

If you have been reading and listening carefully up to this point, it should not be hard to see the parallel between Lady Wisdom and Christ. Like Lady Wisdom, Christ is calling to every human being. He goes to every country, to every city and village, to every home and apartment, and even to the homeless on the street, calling out each person by name: "Stop what you are doing! Listen to my words of wisdom. I have something extremely valuable to offer you. It is worth more than all this world's riches. It is worth more than anything you ever desired. My offer will change your life forever."

Just like Lady Wisdom's offer, Christ's is much needed by every human being. Our sinful lives need Christ's radical, life-changing plan of salvation. As Jesus said to Nicodemus, "If you believe in God's Son, you 'shall not perish but have eternal life'" (John 3:16).

Since the early days of Christianity, some theologians have tried to *equate* Lady Wisdom with Christ, for there are many similarities. Waltke identifies them as follows:

- Both existed with God before all things.
- Both played some role in creation.
- Both descended from heaven to dwell with humanity and were rejected by the masses.
- Both teach heavenly wisdom.
- Both call those who listen "children."

- Both lead those who listen to life and immortality and threaten death to those who do not.
- Both offer blessings in the symbols of food and drink. (2004, 130)

We could also add that both Lady Wisdom and Christ are evangelists, both speak with authority, and both promise that if we seek them, we will find them (Prov. 8:17; Matt. 7:7-8).

However, there are also some significant differences:

- God gave birth to wisdom, but Christ is the eternal Son.
- Wisdom witnessed the creation, but Christ is the Creator.
- Wisdom will laugh at the time of judgment, but Christ is the Judge.
- Wisdom was begotten by God, but Christ is God. (Waltke 2004, 131)

One other difference is even more significant to us because it concerns the forgiveness of our sins. Because Christ died on the cross and rose again, he provides salvation to those who believe in him, whereas Lady Wisdom can only point people to God and her words of wisdom.

This being the case, Christ is clearly superior to Lady Wisdom. Still, we should not diminish her role in leading people to lives of godly wisdom and order. Before Christ came, she spoke for God, calling people to wake up and change. Her message was not quite the same as Christ's because she was not the Son of God. Nevertheless, she clearly prefigured Christ in being "the way and the truth and the life" (John 14:6) for generations of ancient people before Christ's incarnation.

So what are you in need of today? Is your life chaotic or ordered? Are your thoughts and actions foolish or wise? Is your heart still guilty of sin, or have your sins been forgiven? Both Lady Wisdom and Christ offer you today something extremely valuable. As Lady Wisdom said, "Nothing you desire can compare with her" (Prov. 8:11). Jesus echoed that thought when he offered to Nicodemus the opportunity to put aside his old ways, thoughts, habits, and desires, and be born again and receive eternal life (John 3:1-21).

Possible Sermon Titles: "What Do You Really Desire Today?" "A Life-Changing Offer from Lady Wisdom," "What Are You Truly Thankful for This Christmas?" "Lady Wisdom's Usefulness to You Today," "Singing the Praises of Lady Wisdom"

Fight of the Ages (Prov. 9:1-6, 13-18)

In 1971, the media billed the heavyweight boxing match between Muhammad Ali and Joe Frazier "the fight of the century." Both fighters had been undefeated in more than twenty-five matches. The event was watched around the world by three hundred million people. Two rematches were scheduled over the next few years, but neither gained the same billing as the first.

The book of Proverbs describes a "fight of the ages" between Lady Wisdom and Lady Foolishness. Proverbs 1:20-33 introduced readers to a character named Lady Wisdom. She was a street preacher, wandering through the city trying to persuade people to abandon their foolish ways, repent of their sins, turn to the Lord, and live lives of wisdom and obedience to God.

Proverbs 3:1-18 listed the rewards Lady Wisdom bestowed on her followers—gifts worth more than silver, gold, and rubies (vv. 14-15). She desired only the best for every human being. Chapter 8 adds to the résumé of Lady Wisdom. She was a prominent society woman, influencing judges and rulers. Her mission was to speak the truth to all who would listen. The sage's most amazing claim is that God created her before anything else and that she helped God with the rest of creation.

Proverbs 9 offers a blow-by-blow account of the knock-down-and-drag-out fight between Lady Wisdom and Lady Foolishness—Wisdom's evil adversary. Both women were prepared to do battle for the attention of everyone in the entire world. They would spare no effort to influence every single person to follow their ways. This was to be the fight of the ages for the souls of humanity.

This is the only chapter in Proverbs in which the two women appear side by side. This gives us the opportunity to evaluate their personalities, their actions, and their desires for all of us. In this sermon, we will examine both women in detail. Let us begin with Lady Wisdom.

The description of Lady Wisdom in Proverbs 9:1-6 begins with the house where she lives. It is a large house with seven pillars—the number seven indicates it was a "perfect house" (Waltke 2004, 433). Houses of ordinary people in the ancient world had only one or two pillars for roof support. This signifies Lady Wisdom's house was a palatial mansion. It contained many rooms, one of which is a large banquet room for entertaining guests.

Serving banquets was one of Lady Wisdom's favorite activities. She liked to feed as many people as possible. To gain a large crowd for her meals, she sent her servant girls everywhere in the city with an invitation: "Let all who are simple come to my house!" (v. 4a). The doors of her banquet hall were open wide to anyone who cared to dine with her. She herself went to the highest point in the city to invite the city leaders, prominent merchants, and religious authorities, who lived in the best part of the city. Everywhere she went, she called out loudly, hoping everyone in the city would hear and heed her invitation.

Lady Wisdom's invitation extended to all, but she especially urged the simpleminded to attend. They were naive and undisciplined, neither all good nor all bad. They wandered through life trying to avoid hard decisions and failing to consider the consequences of their choices. They were headed for hard times because they refused to make good choices.

The people who responded to Lady Wisdom's invitation were richly rewarded with a delicious meal of elaborately prepared food and drinks. Exquisite meat was on the menu, and wine was lavishly available. The tables were elegantly set. Fellowship with Lady Wisdom was enlightening; her knowledge and insights about life were invaluable; her wisdom was practical and true. The guests who left her banquet were well prepared for life. By the end of the banquet, she had given her guests every valid reason for choosing wisdom as the guiding principle for their lives.

However, another woman also offered banquets in the city of life. Her activities are described in 9:13-18. Her name is Lady Foolishness. Her house was in the nicest part of town—at the highest point in the city. Apparently, she kept company with the city leaders, so her message would seem respectable. She frequently crossed paths with Lady Wisdom.

The sage offers no description of Lady Foolishness's house or the meal she has prepared. This leaves the impression that her house and meal were not as nice as Lady Wisdom's. All we know is that she presented the same invitation: "Let all who are simple come to my house!" (v. 16). To compensate for her lack of elegance, she offered her invited guests an added enticement. She admitted that her food was stolen. Because it was acquired illegitimately, it needed to be eaten in secret. This made it all the more desirable, sweet, and delicious. The implication is that people would be attracted by her appeal to do something shady and immoral. Thus they would prefer her banquet to Lady Wisdom's. Lady Foolishness never mentioned the consequences of attending her banquet, but the author does.

First, her guests would learn absolutely nothing about how to navigate life. Their hostess had nothing to share with them; she was just as simpleminded as the other people attending.

Second, those who came to Lady Foolishness's house were in mortal danger of losing their lives. Many of her guests never left. They died, and their corpses are stacked in a back room waiting to be shuffled off to burial. When they entered her house, they were unaware that her back door leads straight to Sheol and separation from God forever.

Lady Foolishness had no wisdom to offer. She had only momentary pleasures, instant gratification, and the thrill of getting away with something wrong. Her appeal was especially attractive to young people, but anyone can fall for it at a weak moment. The problem was that her pleasures were short lived. Her guests had no future, meaningful life.

So whose house would you like to visit? Which banquet will you attend? The author has skillfully presented an allegory on the ways of life. We all begin simpleminded, just like the guests invited to the banquets of Lady Wisdom and Lady Foolishness. We are ordinary people going about our normal life's activities, minding our own business, simply trying to go to school or earn a living, raise a family, and enjoy good times with family and friends.

As we wander down "Decision Street," it looks familiar—like other streets we have traveled. But we notice that there are only two houses on this street. They sit opposite each other. One house is a huge mansion. The person who lives there has obviously invested a great deal in her house and treated it with care. It has Lady Wisdom's name displayed prominently at the entrance. The owner invites us to come inside where we can enjoy a magnificent banquet and receive top-notch advice on decisions we need to make in life. We already know that the lady of the house has a reputation for being extremely wise about the ways of life. Her recommendations have never been wrong. Everyone who enters her house leaves a better person.

On the opposite side of the street sits a more modest house. The lady of the house is smothered in showy makeup and seductively clothed. She too invites us to a meal. It will not be an extravagant banquet, but the entertainment will get your attention: nightclub-like flashing lights, loud music, raunchy jokes, and popular entertainers. No one will know who her guests are, because there are no windows to her house. Once her guests enter, few leave. They become attracted to her lifestyle and end up staying until they have destroyed themselves.

Lady Wisdom invites her guests to leave behind their old selves with their naive, simpleminded thinking and self-centered lifestyles. They are invited to become new creations, guided by godly principles that have endured the test of time.

Lady Foolishness's invitation is a call to turn aside from a humdrum, ordinary life and enjoy some momentary pleasures. She invites guests to put some excitement in their lives, but the end result will be spiritual death. There you have it—the ultimate choice is between life and death.

The message Proverbs 9 wants to teach us is the same that Jesus taught. There are only two ways to live—build your life on a solid rock, or you will be building it on sand. The next storm will determine whether you are a wise builder or not. And storms will come.

God offered Adam and Eve a choice of trees. They chose the wrong one. Abraham offered his nephew Lot a choice about where to live. He chose the wrong place. Jesus offered the rich, young ruler a choice about priorities. He chose the wrong one.

God offers each of us a choice too. He offers us a rich life, a meaningful life, a life of great wisdom, a life that can draw upon the resources of heaven for strength and security. But Satan is doing everything in his power to draw us the other way. He offers us enticements that seem attractive and exciting but lead nowhere we really want to go. They lead to spiritual death and maybe even an early physical death. Folks, it is time to make a serious choice about where we will dine. In which house will it be?

Possible Sermon Titles: "Life or Death?" "Lady Wisdom vs. Lady Foolishness," "Which Banquet Do You Want to Attend?" "Two Ladies in Your Life: To Whom Will You Give Your Attention?"

III. INDIVIDUAL SAYINGS ATTRIBUTED TO SOLOMON (PROV. 10:1–22:16)

The third division of Proverbs is the largest in the book. It is an eclectic collection of 375 one-line sayings. The editorial heading in Proverbs 10:1 attributes all of these sayings to Solomon. We may further divide these into two sections based on the different form and content of the sayings in 10:1–15:33 compared to 16:1–22:16. Antithetic parallelism is predominant in the first section but is rare in the second. This suggests that the two sections "existed as independent collections before being combined" (Hartley 2016, 119).

There is no obvious organization to the sayings in this division. Each verse stands on its own with no relation to the verses on either side. Preachers can choose their text in any order, without concern for taking it out of context. Probably the best way to deal with one-verse texts is to broaden the context by adding other verses in Proverbs on the same topic (→ my earlier suggestions in the introduction, p. 13; see Pippert 2003 and other commentaries that bring multiple passages together on a single topic). I attempt to do this with each of the sermons in this division. I have chosen several that illustrate some of the main themes in Proverbs.

Advice for Children (Prov. 10:1)

When thinking about parent-child relationships, we usually place the emphasis on the impact that parents have on their children. This impact is substantial and necessary. The sages believed that parents who fear the Lord, who instruct their children in the ways of wisdom, who discipline their children when appropriate, and who make their children proud of them will be rewarded with joy over their children's successes in life (Prov. 22:6; 23:24-25) (→ see later sermon "Advice for Parents," p. 123). On the other hand, parents who do not fear the Lord and do not take seriously their responsibility to train their children will experience grief and heartache (11:29; 17:21, 25; 19:13, 18; 22:15; 23:13-14; 29:15, 17).

However, Proverbs places far more emphasis on the impact children have on their parents. Almost 150 sayings are directed to children and young people. They include vital life lessons children should learn, bad people and situations they should avoid, the importance of obeying one's parents, the joy or grief children can bring to their parents, and the absolute importance of fearing God and seeking wisdom.

Because of this strong emphasis on children, a series of sermons from Proverbs should include at least one sermon dealing with the various words of advice the sages directed to young people. The authors and editors who put this book together intended it to be a guidebook for successful living. Young people are to read it and put its instructions and advice into practice.

The sages used several methods to grab the attention of young people. First, they used *exhortations* addressed to "my son" (e.g., 1:8, 10; 2:1). These didactic sayings offer parental guidance on specific topics. Second, some sayings make *comparisons* between wise children and foolish ones (e.g., 10:1, 5; 13:1). These are not so much exhortations as they are wise insights into what makes young people successful. Third, they employ *longer instructions* on specific topics, such as peer pressure (→ sermon "Peer Pressure," p. 37) or sexual temptation (→ sermon "Lady Foolishness Has Her Eyes on You," p. 65). This sermon, which considers both exhortations and comparative sayings, might be appropriate for a Sunday youth emphasis.

In Proverbs, two themes about child-parent relationships are frequently emphasized. First, children should seek to live lives of wisdom. Second, children should heed the instructions of their parents. Both of these themes appear in our text:

A wise son brings joy to his father,
> but a foolish son brings grief to his mother. (10:1)

In this verse, the terms "father" and "mother" are in synonymous parallelism, meaning that *both* parents are impacted positively and negatively by their children's choices and behavior. The terms "wise son" and "foolish son" are antithetical (opposites), as are "joy" and "grief." All children are categorized as either wise or foolish. Their wisdom or folly was not predestined, but the result of choices God freely granted all humans when he created them with a free will.

1. Seek to Live a Life of Wisdom

The characteristics of a life of wisdom were described in an earlier sermon (→ "How to Be Successful and Wise," ch. 1, p. 27). All the principles discussed there are implied in the term "wise son." Wise young people possess the following traits:

- They fear the Lord.
- They understand human existence from God's point of view.
- They live ordered lives, daily applying wise and godly principles of behavior, in conformity to the will of God.
- They have learned how to discipline themselves for the purpose of pleasing God.
- They listen to the teachings of their parents and heed their advice.
- They seek to gain new knowledge about God and wisdom.
- They bring joy to their parents.

Likewise, all the principles in the earlier sermon "Not All Fools Are the Same" (ch. 2, p. 46) are implied in the term "foolish son." Foolish young people are characterized as follows:

- They have rejected God or see him as irrelevant to their lives.
- They refuse to live by the standards of behavior God desires.
- They think they know it all but lack essential knowledge about life.
- They are morally unprepared to face life's temptations.
- They have rejected any type of discipline that would hinder their free expression.
- They focus only on their own personal gratification.
- They love to stir up strife.
- They refuse to listen to their parents' advice.
- They bring grief to their parents.

Again and again, Proverbs exhorts young people to choose a life of wisdom over a life of foolishness.

2. Heed Your Parents' Advice

All species of the animal kingdom come into this world with a need to learn about life. Some have to learn it pretty much on their own through instinct and the school of hard knocks. These young creatures are often born in great numbers, but they may have a short lifespan because of lurking predators. Other creatures have months or years of support from their parents. This gets them started on the right path. Whether it is lion cubs needing to learn how to hunt or baby birds needing instructions in how to fly or young fish needing help in how to hide from larger fish, all creatures need some basic lessons in survival skills.

Human beings need the support of their parents for the first eighteen or so years of their lives. Most parents take this responsibility seriously and do their best to raise their children properly (Prov. 13:24). As a result, most children appreciate their parents' help, even though they may not express it verbally until later. Proverbs makes it absolutely clear *why* children need the advice of their parents.

First, all children are undisciplined when they are born. Proverbs 22:15 says that "folly is bound up in the heart of a child." That is, children are "born with bad inclinations" (Fox 2009, 703) (see Gen. 8:21; Ps. 51:5 [7 HB]). They will follow these inclinations if their parents do not intervene through education, discipline, and training starting at an early age.

Where did we get the phrase "the terrible twos"? It did not come from a pediatrician's theory about child development. It came from the fact that two-year-old children are going through a phase of life that is often extremely difficult for new parents. Children at that age begin to have a mind of their own. The exercise of their free will often leads to conflicts. They desperately need good parents who will patiently help them develop a sense of order and direction in their lives. Children whose parents fail to do this are headed for a life of calamity (Prov. 3:35; 20:20; 29:15, 17; 30:17).

Second, all children are sinful by nature. We all are born with what theologians call original sin. We have a natural bent toward sinning. Just as Adam and Eve sinned, all human beings continue their rebellious pattern. There is irrefutable experiential evidence that all humans are born self-centered and prone to sin. Our inborn sinfulness becomes evident to everyone around us at an early age. As Proverbs 20:11 says,

Even children make themselves known by their acts,
by whether what they do is pure and right. (NRSV)

Children need parents to teach them what constitutes sin, how to live a life that is pleasing to God, and how to resist and defeat temptation.

Third, all children are ignorant of what previous generations of humanity discovered about life. They need training to learn how to tie their shoes, to ride a bike, to make friends, to solve problems, to deal with disappointments and loss, and so on.

Some life lessons will be taught in school, but the most important ones are learned at home. In 4:1-9, a father tells his sons that he is teaching them the same things that he learned from his own father many years earlier. He was once a child and ignorant of many things in life, but *his father* took the time to instruct him and prepare him for dealing with life issues. Now he fervently urges his sons never to forsake the lessons that were handed down to him (vv. 2, 4-6). "Take hold of my words," he says. Grasp them "with all your heart" (v. 4).

There is a strong sense of intergenerational relationships in the book of Proverbs. The sages believed that we all need lessons from the past to be successful in the present. They also believed that parents are the best conveyors of truth about the past. Thus we need to listen to them and heed their teachings.

American culture, with its sense of personal independence and its constant striving after the latest trend, has much to learn from the OT about the importance of connections with the past, especially one's family's history and values.

I have been continually amazed by the shock many celebrities experience when their family's history is exposed by Henry Louis Gates Jr. on the TV program *Finding Your Roots*. Apparently, their parents and grandparents never thought it was important to pass down to the next generation the heritage and values of their family.

If you are a young person today and your parents and grandparents have never shared that information with you, ask them about it. In a few years, they will be gone and their stories will be lost forever.

For these three reasons, children should listen to the two people who gave them life and heed their advice. Sadly, not all children do this. Here are three biblical examples of children who brought grief and heartache to their parents: Hophni and Phinehas, the sons of Eli (1 Sam. 2:12-25, 27-36; 3:11-14; 4:1-11); Joel and Abijah, the sons of Samuel (8:1-5); and Amnon and Absalom, the sons of David (2 Sam. 13:1-22; 15:1-37; 18:31-33).

Proverbs also offers examples of young people who turned against their parents and caused them pain. Some children have chosen to despise their parents. They mock and ridicule them to their friends (13:1; 15:20; 30:17). Some children have rejected their parents' discipline by turning to a life of laziness—refusing to do their homework and household chores, such as cleaning their rooms (10:5). Some have rejected their parents' godliness and chosen for themselves the life of a godless fool (17:21; 19:13). Some children have cursed their parents to their faces (20:20; 30:11-14). Some have robbed their parents (19:26; 28:24).

Sadly, there are modern examples of adult children putting their elderly parents into nursing homes in order to clean out their bank accounts. Some children, like the prodigal son (Luke 15), have taken their inheritance and squandered it on sinful pleasures and prostitutes (Prov. 23:26-28; 29:3).

Sin gets pretty ugly when it infects family relationships. It drives people apart. It stifles love. It brings embarrassment and shame to parents and anger and hatred to young people. In every proverb that addresses the issue of rebellious young people, the results are the same—shame and embarrassment for the parents and calamity for their children (10:1, 5; 15:20; 17:21, 25; 19:26; 20:20; 28:7, 24; 29:3; 30:17).

Before concluding this sermon/lesson, we should note that in all their admonitions about obeying one's parents, the sages were basically only reinforcing the fifth commandment: "Honor your father and your mother, as the LORD your God has commanded you, so that you may live long and that it may go well with you in the land the LORD your God is giving you" (Deut. 5:16; also Exod. 20:12). By including so many sayings on child-parent relationships, the sages highlighted the significance and meaning of honoring parents as stated in the fifth commandment.

What does the word "honor" mean to you? We know what "dishonor" looks like because the sages spoke about it frequently (see above). It means to despise, mock, ridicule, treat lightly, insult, or reject the authority and discipline of one's parents. It is to curse and rob them.

"Honor," on the other hand, means to respect, to treat with dignity, to hold in high regard, to think highly of one's parents. It means to have a good attitude toward them and to express that attitude through both speech and actions. Such an attitude toward one's parents is pleasing to God according to the Ten Commandments. It will not only bring the parents joy instead of shame but also grant their children long and blessed lives (Prov. 23:15-16, 24-25; 27:11).

This does not mean that children should mindlessly obey their parents in all situations. Some parents are unwise. They abuse their children by treating them harshly, demanding blind obedience, and bringing them into harm's way. Such behavior is abhorrent to God. Parents should stand in for God as symbols of both love and authority; they should exemplify God's gracious behavior before their children. They should honor God in their own lives. Parents with a misguided, selfish agenda are unworthy of obedience from their children.

There are ways for children to deal with this type of dysfunctional family situation. But that is a topic for another sermon. Fortunately, most parents seek the best for their children and do not just order them around like slaves. Most Christian parents try to exemplify God's love in their own lives before their children.

In Ephesians 6:1-4, Paul explains the reason why the fifth commandment needs to be obeyed. It is "right," he says, to honor your father and mother. It is correct. This is how God intended for families to function, and it is pleasing to him when families do so (Col. 3:20).

Paul also notes that the fifth commandment is the first commandment with a promise (Eph. 6:2). A long, enjoyable life is the reward for children who honor and obey their parents. There may be a subtle application to the parents as well. If the children honor their parents, then the parents also have the opportunity for a long and good life. But if the children do not honor them, it is not likely that the parents will enjoy their later years.

What have we learned in this sermon/lesson?

- Early parental training is significant in helping children become wise and successful (Prov. 22:6).
- Children who develop a love for wisdom will be successful (4:5-9; 29:3).
- Children who are obedient to their parents' teachings will do well in life (4:1-4; 28:7).
- Children who practice a disciplined lifestyle are pleasing to God (10:17).
- Children who appropriate God's grace into their lives can grow up to be transformed people who are righteous, holy, redeemed, and wise (1 Cor. 1:26-31), for God "can mold ordinary people and families into great ones" (Van Leeuwen 1997, 5:190).

In conclusion, as a young person, are you facing a situation in your home right now that needs God's help? Are things not going well? Are harsh words becoming more frequent? Are there acts of deliberate disobedience? Do you find yourself criticizing your parents more and more?

Maybe you really want to do something about it but do not know where to start. The place to begin is by acknowledging God as the Lord of your life. Take yourself off the throne of your life. Allow God to manage your anger by letting him become your Savior and Lord. Make God the president of your life, not just a resident on the periphery. Then ask God to give you the courage to say to your parents, "I'm sorry. I really do love and appreciate you. I'd like to push the reset button in our relationship. I'd really like to talk about what's bothering me. I'd like to give you a hug, but I don't know how to do it." I do not know of any parents who would refuse that kind of request.

Possible Sermon Titles: "Children Who Make Their Parents Proud," "Bringing Joy to Your Parents," "How to Get Along with Your Parents," "Relationships in the Home from a Child's Point of View"

Let's Hear It for Common Sense (Prov. 14:20)

In 1776, Thomas Paine published a small pamphlet titled *Common Sense.* In it, he presented several well-reasoned arguments for why the American colonies should revolt against Great Britain. He argued that considering how Great Britain was treating the colonies, it was just common sense for them to declare their independence. The pamphlet was circulated widely in the colonies. It became one of the significant influences leading up to the writing of the Declaration of Independence and the American Revolutionary War.

What do we mean by "common sense"? We hear that term used quite frequently, but what does it really mean? "Common sense" refers to good judgments and sensible practices that are widely shared within a given population. Here are some modern examples: (1) It's common sense that inattentive driving will probably lead to an accident. (2) It's common sense that exercise and a balanced diet will probably lengthen your lifespan. (3) It's common sense that preventative measures taken against disease will probably help people avoid getting sick.

In ancient times, common sense was one of the authorities the sages appealed to in fashioning their books of proverbs and instructional literature. An ancient saying from the Mesopotamian Counsels of Wisdom (fifteenth c. BC) illustrates this:

Do not set out to stand around in the assembly.
Do not loiter where there is a dispute,
For in the dispute they will have you as an *observer*.
Then you will be made a witness for them, and
They will involve you in a lawsuit to affirm something that does
    not concern you.
In case of a dispute, get away from it, disregard it. (*ANET*, 595,
    ll. 31-37)

The point of this saying is simply, "Stay away from disputes that do not involve you." It is a commonsense word of advice to warn people of the dangers of becoming trapped in other people's quarrels.

The biblical sages also appealed to common sense. They believed there were sound principles of order that God had written into the very fabric of life. These should be obvious to everyone. If we intend to live well and avoid as many problems of life as possible, we should be aware of this order and act accordingly. The proverb I have chosen to illustrate this is Proverbs 14:20:

The poor are shunned even by their neighbors,
    but the rich have many friends.

This proverb states a sad fact about life that is self-evident. Poor people have few friends. Rich people have many. The proverb does not state the reason for this, but most people figure it out. The poor have little to offer others, while the rich have more than enough. Humans gravitate toward those who can enrich their lives. We shun the poor, not just because they have nothing to offer us, but because we rationalize the cause of their poverty is "laziness or lack of intelligence" (Hartley 2016, 163). We do not want to be identified with people who are lazy or stupid. Of course, such reasoning is false. Poverty can arise from many other factors, such as the loss of employment, losses due to accidents or natural disasters, extended illness, systemic racism or ethnic and cultural prejudice, and generational dysfunction.

The present proverb simply recognizes a social reality, neither endorsing nor condemning it: Society treats the poor and the rich differently. The sages are not making a value judgment. They merely call attention to an issue that exists in all societies.

Other proverbs do render value judgments about poverty, for example, in the next verse:

It is a sin to despise one's neighbor,

but blessed is the one who is kind to the needy. (v. 21)

This proverb resembles a prophetic call for social justice (consider Amos 2:6-7 or Isa. 10:1-4). It pronounces a divine blessing on those who heed the challenging words. However, Proverbs contains few of such sayings.

More frequent are commonsense proverbs, which offer candid observations about how life works. Let us consider some of the ways the sages taught their students to use common sense in making important decisions in life.

1. It Is Common Sense That Some Situations in Life Are Self-Evident

In addition to our text (Prov. 14:20), here are some other examples:

Those who work their land will have abundant food,

but those who chase fantasies have no sense. (12:11)

An honest witness tells the truth,

but a false witness tells lies. (v. 17)

Anxiety weighs down the heart,
>   but a kind word cheers it up. (v. 25)

Light in a messenger's eyes brings joy to the heart,
>   and good news gives health to the bones. (15:30)

The wealth of the rich is their fortified city;
>   they imagine it a wall too high to scale. (18:11)

In a lawsuit the first to speak seems right,
>   until someone comes forward and cross-examines. (v. 17)

"It's no good, it's no good!" says the buyer—
>   then goes off and boasts about the purchase. (20:14)

Rich and poor have this in common:
>   The Lord is the Maker of them all. (22:2)

In each of these proverbs, no explanation was needed because the meaning was obvious. Everyone recognized the truthfulness of each. This is just the way life is.

What was the purpose of these proverbs? Why do we need to know that honest people tell the truth and dishonest people lie (12:17)? That good news cheers up our spirits (15:30)? That bargain hunters have a different attitude after they have purchased something than before (20:14)?

The sages simply wanted to reveal what life is like. If you believe that God ordered the world he created, then it is important to know what that order is. If you know what that order is, then you can arrange your life to fit God's plans and you can live a successful life.

The book of Job takes a similar approach in discussing the members of the animal kingdom (38:39–39:30; 40:15–41:34). The appearance and behavior of each kind of animal is different from those of other kinds of animals. God has ordered their characteristics that way. We can understand these animals better if we observe them and discover the order that God has established.

Here are examples of modern proverbs that similarly seek to reveal simple, self-evident truths about life:

- A rolling stone gathers no moss.
- Birds of a feather flock together.

- A stitch in time saves nine.

2. It Is Common Sense That Some Situations in Life Are Caused by Others

Cause-and-effect reasoning was another way the sages explained situations in life. Sometimes one thing comes before another and causes the second to happen. The two situations are thus linked in a causative relationship. Here are some examples:

A wise son brings joy to his father,
> but a foolish son brings grief to his mother (10:1).

Walk with the wise and become wise,
> for a companion of fools suffers harm. (13:20)

Pride goes before destruction,
> a haughty spirit before a fall. (16:18)

A cheerful heart is good medicine,
> but a crushed spirit dries up the bones. (17:22)

A little sleep, a little slumber,
> a little folding of the hands to rest—
and poverty will come on you like a thief
> and scarcity like an armed man. (24:33-34)

What causes some people to fail in life and others to succeed? We all need to know to prevent failure in our own lives. The sages had observed that false pride and a haughty spirit sometimes caused people's downfall (16:18). For other people, their choice of friends and associates was the determining factor. Wisdom and success in life are gained by associating with wise people (13:20).

Proverbs 17:22 describes how our attitudes affect our physical condition. A cheerful disposition contributes to good health, while depression may result in physical aches and pains. The point of the proverb is to encourage people to develop good attitudes, for their attitudes will affect their health and appearance.

There are several places in Scripture where the imagery of reaping and sowing are connected in a causal relationship using proverbs. The most well known is Paul's instructions in Galatians 6:7-9. Others are found in Job 4:8; Proverbs 22:8; Hosea 8:7; 10:12; 2 Corinthians 9:6.

In Jeremiah 31:29 and Ezekiel 18:2, the prophets describe how the Jewish exiles tried to blame the previous generation for their exile to Babylon. They would quote this proverb:

The parents have eaten sour grapes,
> and the children's teeth are set on edge. (Jer. 31:29)

They denied responsibility for their unpleasant situation. They blamed their parents for the disaster. In this case, there was no cause-and-effect relationship to other people. God will punish all people for their own sins (Ezek. 18:3-4).

Here are two modern proverbs that use cause-and-effect reasoning to teach two commonsense truths about life:

- Absence makes the heart grow fonder.
- An apple a day keeps the doctor away.

3. It Is Common Sense That Some Situations in Life Are like Others

The sages were always looking for ways to explain something odd, inconsistent, or unknown. To do this they often turned to analogies. They would place something understandable alongside something confusing to see if they could use one to explain the other. Here is an example:

As the heavens are high and the earth is deep,
> so the hearts of kings are unsearchable. (Prov. 25:3)

What does the height of heaven and the depth of the earth have to do with the mind of a king? Not much really. Yet the bringing of the two together illustrates how useless it is to try to predict what a king (or any government official) will do. Just as we are ignorant of many things in the far reaches of the sky or the depths of the earth, so we will always be puzzled by the decisions rulers make.

Other proverbs similarly use analogies to explain odd situations:

Like clouds and wind without rain
> is one who boasts of gifts never given. (25:14)

Like a city whose walls are broken through
> is a person who lacks self-control. (v. 28)

Like one who grabs a stray dog by the ears
>   is someone who rushes into a quarrel not their own. (26:17)

Like a coating of silver dross on earthenware
>   are fervent lips with an evil heart. (v. 23)

As iron sharpens iron,
>   so one person sharpens another. (27:17)

Death and Destruction are never satisfied,
>   and neither are human eyes. (v. 20)

For as churning cream produces butter,
>   and as twisting the nose produces blood,
>   so stirring up anger produces strife. (30:33)

Here is an analogy from Ezekiel that explains why the people of Jerusalem acted so sinfully: "Everyone who quotes proverbs will quote this proverb about you: 'Like mother, like daughter'" (Ezek. 16:44). Here are two similar modern proverbs:

- He's a chip off the old block.
- Time and tide wait for no one.

4. **It Is Common Sense That Some Situations in Life Are Better than Others**

Here are some examples:

Better a little with the fear of the LORD
>   than great wealth with turmoil. (Prov. 15:16)

Better a small serving of vegetables with love
>   than a fattened calf with hatred. (v. 17)

Better to be lowly in spirit with the oppressed
>   than to share plunder with the proud. (16:19)

Better to meet a bear robbed of her cubs
>   than a fool bent on folly (17:12).

Do not exalt yourself in the king's presence,
>   and do not claim a place among his great men;
> it is better for him to say to you, "Come up here,"

than for him to humiliate you before his nobles. (25:6-7; cf. Luke 14:10)

As with analogies, the sages set two situations side by side but in this case claimed one to be better than the other. The sages made value judgments about choosing between two viable courses of action. They did not explain why one option was better than the other. Apparently, long experience had proven one option preferable.

Proverbs 15:16-17 deals with the issue of wealth versus poverty. Which would you rather have? Of course, everyone wants wealth. But what if wealth came with the price of turmoil and hatred? Which option would you choose then? Here the sages stressed that poverty may not be so bad after all if wealth resulted in quarreling and the disruption of one's social relationships.

Here are two modern proverbs that make similar value judgments between two situations:

- Better late than never.
- A bird in the hand is worth two in the bush.

5. It Is Common Sense That All People Should Fear the Lord

Perhaps the most important sayings in the book of Proverbs are those that deal with morality—those that emphasize the importance of a relationship with God and righteous living. God is not mentioned by name in most of the sayings in Proverbs, but he does appear in some. In the others, he is the underlying foundation and overall background of every discussion. His ordering of the world at the time of creation is what gives meaning to the hundreds of sayings. Those sayings provide direction for the lives of all human beings. They lead to successful living. The most obvious verse dealing with morality is the theme verse:

The fear of the LORD is the beginning of knowledge,

but fools despise wisdom and instruction. (Prov. 1:7)

Many similar verses appear throughout the book. Without question, reverencing and obeying God lies at the heart of the sages' teaching about what constitutes good living. The modern proverb of eighteenth-century philosopher Voltaire explains why so many people fail to act logically: "Common sense is not so common."

Let us look at what the sages meant by the phrase "the fear of the LORD." Fourteen verses in Proverbs contain the phrase "the fear of the LORD" (*yir'at YHWH*). Five additional verses associate the verb "fear" (*yr'*) with *YHWH* (Yahweh). Three concepts are implied.

First, fearing the Lord always involves consciously placing God in an exalted position of awe and reverence. As the first commandment states, "You shall have no other gods before me" (Exod. 20:3). For the Israelites, this commandment usually meant rejecting the pagan gods of the foreign nations around them and of the Canaanites living among them. In addition, it also required them to accept Yahweh as the only deity in existence. He was a unique, universal God who had demonstrated his interest in all human beings by creating them, ordering their world, sustaining their world, and continuing to speak to them in their own languages. Therefore, he deserved and continues to deserve reverence and respect from all humanity. In fact, we should be zealous for God and his plans for us (Prov. 23:17). When Americans say the pledge of allegiance, they are committing their loyalty to one country—the United States of America. God deserves and wants that same kind of allegiance—no other gods in addition to him.

This theology is not spelled out in the book of Proverbs, but it is found in other parts of the OT (Deut. 6:4; Ps. 81:9-10 [10-11 HB]; Isa. 44:6; 45:5-6; Hos. 13:4-6) and in the NT (Matt. 4:10; 6:24; Mark 12:28-34; 1 Cor. 8:4-6). The sages were aware of this theology when they encouraged people to fear the Lord.

Second, fearing the Lord always meant submitting one's life to God. One could not be self-centered and fear the Lord (Prov. 3:7). Self-interest can never preempt God and his plans for our lives. Humility before God is the proper characteristic of those who fear the Lord (15:33; 22:4).

Third, fearing the Lord always affects our behavior. On the positive side, fearing the Lord meant "doing what is right and just and fair" (1:3; see 14:2). This required earnestly seeking God's wisdom and instructions for our lives (2:1-5). On the negative side, it meant rejecting evil and all evil practices. These included pride, arrogance, perverse speech (8:13); devious ways (14:2); and hotheadedness (v. 16). Evil is not even to be considered or envied by those who fear the Lord (23:17).

The sages were aware that fearing the Lord was a conscious choice that all people must make for themselves (1:29). It was not an easy choice, for Lady Foolishness was constantly trying to tempt people to choose another way (7:6-27; 9:13-18). Nevertheless, fearing the Lord was an achievable way of life for those who seriously applied their hearts to seek it as diligently as they would search for hidden treasure (2:1-5).

The reason sages urgently called people to fear the Lord was that the results of this choice had far-reaching consequences. Some of the benefits they listed were wisdom and knowledge (9:10), long life (10:27), security from life's troubles (14:26; 19:23; 24:21-22; 29:25), "riches and honor and life" (22:4), and God's blessing (28:14) (→ additional rewards in the earlier sermon "Wisdom's Rewards," p. 51). Some of these rewards may be modified due to other circumstances. However, the overall lesson from the sages was that life would go much better for us if we feared the Lord. To do so was merely to align one's life with undeniable reality. They considered it common sense that all people should fear the Lord.

In conclusion, I challenge you to think about two questions: First, is there anything or anyone that you think of more highly than God? It could be your family, your business or occupation, your well-being, your popularity, your political interests, your hobbies and entertainment, and so on. If so, the sages have a commonsense word of wisdom for you: You need to lower its importance and raise God to his rightful, supreme place in your heart!

Second, is there anything or anyone that has come between you and God's plans for your life? If so, the sages have a commonsense word of wisdom for you: Put it aside and seek God's wisdom for your life!

In other words, you need to fear the Lord. It is such a commonsense decision. You will be extremely and eternally glad you did.

Possible Sermon Titles: "Commonsense Theology," "The Sages' Commonsense Approach to Life"

The Power of the Tongue (Prov. 18:21)

I began writing this sermon about a year and a half into the COVID-19 pandemic. The first week of the 2021-22 school year was just around the corner for most schoolchildren in our community. For several months, TV reporters had been covering the heated meetings at local school boards. Angry parents who wanted the school board to make masks optional in school often disrupted these meetings. They thought they had a right to send their unvaccinated children to school without a mask, even if by doing so they could infect other children with the virus. Just as passionate were fearful parents on the other side who were insistent that masks should be required for everyone to protect their unvaccinated children from this deadly disease. They threatened to take their children out of school if the school board did not require masks. Parents of disabled children tried to point out that their children could not even go to school if masks were not required of everyone. These meetings were no-win situations for school board members who simply wanted to provide a good education for all children.

Watching these events transpire on TV reminded me of how powerful our speech is. Some of the speeches I heard were totally illogical, poorly worded, and sadly disrespectful. They would have failed in any speech class. But their volume and emotional delivery won the support of many in the room.

Considering the way people speak out today, both orally and over the internet, a sermon on our speech is surely a useful topic in any series of sermons based on Proverbs. The ancient sages of Israel were aware of the power of words. It was important to them that people took care in what they said. They included over 125 proverbs in the book that deal with speech. Many more do not specifically mention speaking but imply that speaking is taking place. Thus many supplemental passages can be used to broaden the meaning of our one-verse text:

The tongue has the power of life and death,

    and those who love it will eat its fruit. (Prov. 18:21)

There are two ideas expressed in this verse. The first part of the verse emphasizes the power of our words *on other people*. The sages here used the "tongue," the most visible organ of human speech, figuratively to refer to what people say. Speech is a very powerful tool given by God to human beings. It can be used to affect other people for good or for evil. Good words are "right," "true," and "just" (8:6-9); nourishing (10:21); "honest" (12:17); "soothing" (15:4); "apt" and "timely" (v. 23); "pure" (v. 26); "gracious," "sweet," and "healing" (16:24); "pleasing" (22:17-18); and "gentle" (25:15). They are compared to a "fountain of life" (10:11), "choice silver" (10:20), honey (16:24), a "rushing stream" (18:4), a "rare jewel" (20:15), and a "kiss on the lips" (24:26). They bring nourishment and blessing to all who hear them.

Examples of the evil use of speech are deceit (3:28), "perversity" (4:24), seduction (7:21), idle "chattering" (10:8, 10), "lying" and "slander" (v. 18), quarreling (17:14, 19; 26:21), "gossip" (18:8), verbal attack (25:18), and dishonest flattery (29:5). Proverbs 25:18 compares bad words to "a club or a sword or a sharp arrow." But the most powerful statement is found in 18:21: "The tongue has the power of life and death."

Evil words can literally cause someone's death. The word "death" may intend more than the cessation of physical life. It could be a figure of speech for the crushing of one's spirit (15:4; 18:14) or the isolation of someone from human society. Job's description of his rejection by his family, friends, and community is as close to death as one can come without actually dying (Job 19:13-20).

Second, Proverbs 18:21 also emphasizes the consequences of speech *on us*. We must live with what we have said. Other people evaluate us by the words that come out of our mouths or that we post on the internet. According to 19:9, lying can lead to punishment and even an early death. How many have been embarrassed by notes posted on social media years earlier? Once something is published on the internet, it is there forever.

Words are powerful. James compares our tongues to a ship's rudder (James 3:4-6). A rudder is a very small but essential part of a ship, used to steer it. The rudder is what turns a huge ship in the direction it needs to go. Similarly, our tongues are quite small, but they wield great power to speak good or evil. We need to control what we say, so that we do not ignite a fire that destroys ourselves and others. Some people's tongues need to be registered "with the authorities as a deadly weapon" (Murphey 2001, 38).

Proverbs 10–15 are known for their overwhelming use of comparative sayings that use antithetic parallelism. The first half of these verses presents a truism, while the second half states its opposite using "but" as the conjunction between the two. A good number of these sayings highlight the differences between good speech and bad speech. Here are some examples:[1]

Good speech produces wisdom.
> But bad speech is silenced. (10:31)

Good speech is honored.
> But bad speech is perverse/false/distorted. (v. 32)

Good speech builds up a city.
> But bad speech destroys it. (11:11)

Bad speech destroys one's neighbors.
> But good speech rescues them. (12:6; see 11:9)

Bad speech brings evil on oneself.
> But good speech escapes this. (12:13)

Good speakers tell the truth.
> But bad speakers tell lies. (v. 17; see 14:5)

Bad speech attacks with swords.
> But good speech brings healing. (12:18; see 13:17)

Good speech lasts forever.
> But bad speech lasts only a moment. (12:19)

God detests bad speech.
> But he delights in good speech. (v. 22)

Good speakers keep their knowledge to themselves.
> But bad speakers blurt out folly. (v. 23)

Good speech produces enjoyable things.
> But bad speech produces violence. (13:2)

Good speakers enjoy a secure life.
> But bad speakers come to ruin. (v. 3; see 14:3)

---

1. The following verses are the author's interpretive translations.

Good speakers save lives.
> But bad speakers spread deceit. (14:25)

Good speech turns away wrath.
> But bad speech stirs up anger. (15:1)

Good speakers seek and produce knowledge.
> But bad speakers seek and produce folly. (v. 2; see vv. 7, 14)

Good speech produces life.
> But bad speech crushes people's spirit. (v. 4)

With these two contrasting thoughts in mind, how should God's people speak? What would the sages want to hear from the mouths of their readers? Here are seven characteristics in Proverbs of the words that should be found on the lips of God's people.

1. Honest and Truthful

Over and over again the sages condemned bad speech, such as lying (Prov. 14:5; 24:12, 24; 26:28; 30:8), deceitfulness (26:18-19, 24-26), flattery (26:28; 29:5), and boasting (27:1-2). God's people should not engage in these practices. Even speech that may not be outright lies, but deceptively sly, should be avoided (25:23). The sages also pointed out certain types of people that are prone to lie—adulterous individuals (5:3-4; 22:14), troublemakers (6:12), enemies (26:24-26; 27:6), and sinners (28:13).

God's people should speak only what is right (23:16). Truthfulness will create the atmosphere for friendships to develop and grow and will allow people to correct each other without creating conflict (27:5-6). God does not expect his people to agree about every issue in life. There will be times of disagreement. Nevertheless, if handled honestly and with restraint, good discussion will actually make each person better:

As iron sharpens iron,
> so one person sharpens another. (v. 17)

Honesty is particularly important in our relationship with God. We can never be completely right with him without confessing all our sins and forsaking our sinful ways (28:13).

The sages recognized that kings wanted those who serve them to be honest (16:13). Every four years, Americans elect a new president. This person then has the awesome task of selecting new cabinet members and appointing thousands of people to positions in the government. The candidates all go through intense probing into their character. Some are confirmed, and some are not. If you were the president and needed to select new cabinet members, what kind of persons would you be looking for? Would you want a talker? Would you want someone who has all the answers? Would you want someone who gives an answer even without knowing what he or she is talking about? Would you want someone who always tries to please and put a good spin on things? If it were me, I would want someone who was completely honest with me, even if it hurt. I would rather have someone who said "I don't know" than someone who tried to manufacture an answer out of ignorance. I would just want to know the facts. Many presidents have been hurt because the people they appointed to help them were not honest. The same would hold true for all employers. They want their employees to be honest and truthful with them. Such employees are "like a kiss on the lips" to their employers (24:26).

2. Wise

Wisdom is not always found in the speeches of public figures. More likely, one hears complaining, accusation, finger pointing, avoidance of responsibility, exaggeration, or downplaying. Our society desperately needs wise speakers—people who have done their homework and really know what is going on, people who can inform the public of important issues that need addressing and work to solve them (Prov. 16:21). Such speakers are a "fountain of life" (13:14), a gushing stream (18:4), and a "rare jewel" (20:15) to society. They bring a sense of satisfaction to the population in general (18:20), leading people away from making disastrous decisions (13:14). Wise speech also needs to be found in private conversations. In 31:26, it is one of the characteristics of the virtuous woman.

3. Calm and Healing

When people discover things they do not like, they sometimes lash out against the perceived source of the problem. However, the sages encouraged people not to speak hastily in response (Prov. 29:20), not to become "hot-tempered" (v. 22), not to be "quarrelsome"

(26:21), and not to stir up anger (30:33). Rather, they should restrain their emotions and seek to speak words of "healing" (12:18; see 15:30; 17:27). Such a response allows all sides to have a fair hearing (18:13) and for tempers to cool (15:1).

We must not think that calm speaking is wimpy and gets nothing accomplished; the sages noted, "a gentle tongue can break a bone" (25:15). It may seem impossible that something as soft as our tongue could shatter a hard bone—but it can. A patient and calm advisor can persuade a ruler to take a particular course of action (v. 15). Calm, healing speech can dissolve tensions and avoid strife. It nourishes our souls (10:21), cheers us up (12:25), and brings "good things" into our lives (v. 14). No wonder it is compared to honey (16:24).

4. Few in Number

Sometimes people talk too much (Prov. 20:19). They think that verbosity is a sign of importance. Their lips are constantly moving. The sages learned to store up knowledge until the proper moment for its revealing (10:14). They guarded their mouths (v. 19; 13:3) and spoke only when necessary (11:12; 17:27). They took time to weigh their answers before speaking (15:28), and they knew how to keep a secret (11:13). They knew that the less you speak, the less you open yourself up to your critics. They had observed that silence often enhances one's reputation as wise. Even fools could look wise, if they kept their mouths shut (17:28). By keeping their words to a minimum, the sages avoided many calamities that befall people (13:14; 21:23). There is one other thought here. People who speak a lot start liking the sound of their voices. Soon they consider themselves important authorities, even though they lack the credentials to be so. Verbosity cannot hide an empty mind or a sinful heart. As the sages noted, "Sin is not ended by multiplying words" (10:19).

5. Appropriate

Knowing what to say and when to say it are skills that we all would like to master because they both have to be correct in order to speak effectively (Prov. 15:23). Sometimes the opportunity is right for us to say something, but we mess up the content. Other times we say the right thing, but our words fail to accomplish anything because we say them too soon or too late. Just as good farmers know the appropriate time for plowing and planting their crops (20:4), so God's people should know the appropriate time for speaking and the appropriate words to say. Even judges are commended when delivering an appropriate ruling. Such rulings are "like apples of gold in settings of silver" (25:11).

How can we learn how to speak more appropriately? First, we must think before we open our mouths. The mouths of fools are like fire hoses that spew folly and evil continually (15:2). The wise and righteous are people who carefully ponder how they should answer before setting their mouths in motion (v. 28). Second, to speak appropriately, God must be our source of wisdom. Only he has the right and best answers. As the sages noted, "For the LORD gives wisdom; from his mouth come knowledge and understanding" (2:6). Third, we must be righteous people of good character. Only the righteous can speak appropriately (4:23-24; 10:31-32). This leads to the next point.

6. Righteous

Righteousness in the wisdom literature refers to the kind of order and behavior that is proper from God's perspective. Job was insistent that he had practiced proper behavior throughout his entire life (Job 27:6). He was figuratively clothed in righteousness (29:14).

The introduction to Proverbs states that one purpose of the book is to teach people what righteous order and behavior look like on a practical level. It teaches what it means for human beings to conform their lives to the will of God (Prov. 1:3). Righteous words are words that are morally right and proper. God likes them because they advance proper order and behavior. The sages described them as words that impart wisdom (10:31) and are "gracious" and "pure" (15:26). They regarded them as extremely valuable, comparing them to "choice silver" and contrasting them with the worthless, perverse words of the wicked (10:20; see vv. 31-32).

Righteous words can only be spoken by those whose hearts are righteous, for our words reflect the spiritual condition of our hearts. Jesus made a similar comment when he was accused of casting out demons by the power of Beelzebul: "Make a tree good and its fruit will be good, or make a tree bad and its fruit will be bad, for a tree is recognized by its fruit. . . . For the mouth speaks what the heart is full of" (Matt. 12:33-34). James 3:9-12 emphasized the same thought. One spring cannot produce both fresh and salt water. Whatever type of water is in the heart of the spring will come out of its mouth.

7. Loving

In addition to being honest, wise, calm, few, appropriate, and righteous, our words should be loving. Proverbs 10:12 and 17:9 deal with our reaction to wrongs that may be committed against us by another. Should a person react with hatred or love? The sages made it clear that hateful words will lead to conflict. Only loving words should come from the mouths of God's people. Those who jump to quick conclusions and spout off malicious and revengeful words against every slight soon find themselves engulfed in verbal attacks and counterattacks.

Love has a way of covering over disagreements and difficult situations. It allows time for tensions to dissipate, hurt feelings to heal, and misunderstandings to be cleared up. Moreover, loving words have to be spoken to be effective. The silent treatment, or "hidden love" (27:5), in reaction to a wrong only increases the possibility of deepening conflict. No doubt, the author of 10:12 was familiar with the admonition in Leviticus 19:18 to love one's neighbor as oneself. If people would really do that, there would be less likelihood of conflicts breaking out.

The NT expands further on loving speech. Paul admonished the Ephesians to speak "the truth in love" (Eph. 4:15). By speaking this way, we will mature into a community worthy to be called Christ's body with Christ as its head. In 1 Corinthians 13:4-7, Paul defined loving words as "patient" and "kind." They do not "envy" or "boast." They are "not proud." They do "not dishonor others." They are "not self-seeking." They are "not easily angered." They keep "no record of wrongs." They do "not delight in evil" but rejoice "with the truth." They always protect, trust, hope, and persevere. Loving speech practices the Golden Rule (Matt. 7:12; Luke 6:31), by building up others (Eph. 4:29), even one's enemies (Matt. 5:43-48).

In conclusion, how has your speaking been going lately? Have you used good words or bad words? How honest, wise, calm, few, appropriate, righteous, and loving have your words been? During this sermon, have you been thinking about the things that you have said this past week to other people? Do you need to apologize for any of the words that you have spoken recently to family and friends? Maybe now is the time to do some personal evaluation of your own speaking habits in the light of the sages' comments in the book of Proverbs. Perhaps your evaluation will reveal that your mouth needs to be submitted to God and cleansed of any filthiness.

The first step to changing our speech must start with our hearts, for as Jesus said, "The mouth speaks what the heart is full of" (Matt. 12:34). Jesus echoed what wisdom writers had said centuries earlier:

Above all else, guard your heart,

for everything you do flows from it.

Keep your mouth free of perversity;

keep corrupt talk far from your lips. (Prov. 4:23-24)

Possible Sermon Titles: "What Are You Saying?" "Can You Hear Me Now?" "Speech Class 101," "The Fundamentals of Speaking Well," "Open Mouth, Insert Foot"

A Good Marriage (Prov. 18:22)

Proverbs has much to say about marriage relationships. Therefore, this might be an appropriate preaching topic for the Sunday before Valentine's Day.

In the OT, the marriage relationship consisted of one man and one woman. There was no discussion of the possibility of gay and lesbian relationships. Neither was there any support for polygamy. It is true that most Israelite kings had more than one wife. Solomon was the extreme example with seven hundred wives plus three hundred concubines (1 Kings 11:3-6). But the text never says, "Go thou and do likewise." In fact, it emphasizes that Solomon's many wives led him away from God. Royal polygamous marriages were probably accepted in Israel only because it was common in royal marriages in other countries. People thought a king's large harem increased his status. In addition, royal families of two countries would marry to establish peace treaties between their realms. This occurred several times during the Israelite monarchy.

It is also true that some ordinary Israelite men had more than one wife. Almost without exception, these extra wives were the result of abnormal situations. Abraham had a child by Hagar, but only after it seemed clear that his first wife, Sarah, could have no children. Jacob had two wives, but only because his father-in-law, Laban, tricked him on his wedding night. Elkanah had two wives, but only because his first wife, Hannah, was barren (1 Sam. 1:1-2). In all these marriages, the intense rivalry between the wives led to conflict.

Levirate marriage came into play when a man died, leaving his wife childless. His brother or the next of kin was responsible for taking the widow as his wife so the dead man's heritage could continue. Again, this was a special circumstance, not the norm. We do not know how frequently levirate marriage occurred. And we have no information about how the addition of a second wife affected the man's relationship with his first wife. So under normal circumstances, the OT supports marriage as a union between one man and one woman.

Old Testament society was patriarchal, but this does not mean that women had no rights. It is true that the parents arranged many marriages. It is also true that young people did not have the same dating privileges as teens today. There is no evidence that girls were bought and sold like cattle in the marketplace. Neither is there evidence that wives were considered slaves, servants, or simply property.

The OT supports the view that both men and women were created equally in the image of God (Gen. 1:27) and that the two of them became a single union when they united in marriage (2:24).

Probably the best saying in Proverbs on the value of marriage is our text for today:

He who finds a wife finds what is good
    and receives favor from the Lord. (18:22)

One of the most enjoyable blessings in life is a good spouse. Of course, not every spouse is good; we will talk about this later. The clear focus of our text is on a good marriage relationship—one in which both partners believe that God has blessed them with a fantastic companion to enjoy for the rest of their lives.

If nothing else, our text indicates that a good marriage is possible. Our world today is saturated with media portrayals of marriages gone wrong and one-night stands. Country-western radio stations fill the air with sad songs about cheating and breakups. Television shows lead people to believe that good relationships can be developed in a few weeks based on passion, physical appearance, and a few shallow conversations. But how many last? The sages believed that good marriages are possible. Indeed, they are valuable treasures. Therefore, young people should be encouraged to ask God to help them find a good spouse and then be a good marriage partner themselves.

There are many passages in Proverbs that help us identify the characteristics of a good marriage. Here are four:

1. A Good Marriage Is a Gift from God

> Houses and wealth are inherited from parents,
>> but a prudent wife is from the LORD. (Prov. 19:14)

Proverbs 19:14 observes that some positive benefits in life are inherited. Money, land, possessions, and businesses can all be passed down from parents to children. However, a good spouse and an enjoyable marriage cannot be inherited. In some cultures, both in ancient and modern times, marriages are arranged by the parents (Gen. 24:3-4; 38:6). This is an attempt by parents to start their children on a good pathway in life. The parents have no control over whether the relationship works out or not. Only the two marriage partners themselves can make a good marriage.

First, a good spouse has to be selected. That is a risky business considering that our lives and life's circumstances change over the lifespan of a marriage. Second, a good marriage requires ongoing work. Only the two individuals involved can decide whether they want to do that. In both cases, we need God's help to make the best decisions (Prov. 8:35; 16:3). Seeking God's advice and making him a legitimate third partner will not always guarantee a successful marriage. However, it will provide a solid foundation for a marriage to build upon and excellent guidance along the way. For this reason, a good marriage is truly a gift from God.

If you have a good spouse, you ought to thank the Lord every day and tell your spouse as well how much you love him or her. You are a fortunate person, because there are so many people today who are trying to survive in marriages that are not happy at all.

2. A Good Marriage Is Founded on a Covenant between Partners

Wisdom will save you also from the adulterous woman,

from the wayward woman with her seductive words,

who has left the partner of her youth

and ignored the covenant she made before God. (Prov. 2:16-17)

Marriage counselors sometimes compare a marriage relationship to a covenant (*bĕrît*). Covenants in the ancient world were formal agreements between two parties concerning obligations that they agreed to keep. Covenants were like ancient treaties between countries. The most important usage of the word "covenant" in the OT is its application to the relationship between God and his chosen people the Israelites. In that case, Yahweh was the senior partner who offered the Israelites his steadfast love and care if they would acknowledge him as their only God and obey the stipulations of the law.

A good marriage functions like a covenant because the two spouses agree to the terms of the marriage vows—promising to love, comfort, honor, and keep each other in good times and in bad, and, forsaking all others, to love and to cherish each other until death causes a separation. In marriage, there is no superior partner as in the OT covenant between God and Israel. Rather, there are two equal partners, each pledging their unconditional love for each other.

One purpose of marriage is to provide help for the other partner. God saw that one person would be very lonely in life and handicapped by what he or she could accomplish. A coequal helper was needed. Adam's response when Eve was presented to him was, "This is now bone of my bones and flesh of my flesh" (Gen. 2:23). This is clearly a covenantal statement, meaning, "We are one. We are joined together in a common endeavor." At the center of this relationship is trust, loyalty, and devotion to one another. Another wisdom writer put it this way: A married couple (1) can get more done than a single person, (2) can pull each other up when one falls down, (3) can warm and encourage each other when one is cold or lonely, and (4) can defend each other when either one is attacked (Eccles. 4:9-12).

3. A Good Marriage Is Built on Noble Character, Wise Decisions, and Working Together

The wise woman builds her house,

> but with her own hands the foolish one tears hers down. (Prov. 14:1)

People of shallow and perverse character do not make good marriage partners. That is something would-be spouses need to think about before they say, "I do."

Several verses in Proverbs address the difficulty of trying to live with a spouse who is unhappy, quarrelsome, never satisfied, nitpicking, constantly complaining, or putting the other person down. It would be better to live in the desert by yourself (21:19) or on a corner of your flat-roofed house (v. 9; 25:24). A quarrelsome spouse is like "the constant dripping of a leaky roof" (19:13; see 27:15-16). The problem is irritating, and it will not go away. It takes two positive, wise, hardworking partners to make a marriage work. Of course, it does not hurt if you are both crazy about each other: "May you ever be intoxicated with her love" (5:19). Every marriage needs some hot romance.

People united in marriage will either make or break the other spouse. A foolish wife will tear her marriage apart, but a wise and noble wife will seek to build hers up (14:1). Proverbs 19:14 describes the wife in a good marriage as "prudent." The virtuous woman in 31:10-31 was one such wife (→ later sermon "A Woman to Be Praised," p. 171). Her contribution to her family was extraordinary—economically, educationally, socially, and spiritually. She was the rock that enabled her marriage and family to function well. She brought her husband "good, not harm," so that he had full confidence in her; he could trust her with managing his household and possessions (vv. 11-12). A noble wife adds so much to her marriage that she can metaphorically be called "her husband's crown" (12:4). The sages encouraged Israelite young men to consider carefully the example of a virtuous woman when selecting the right young woman as their spouse (6:20-24; 31:10-31).

4. Good Marriage Partners Know the Value of Discipline

Good marriage partners work together to improve their lives, making time for each other and enjoying each other's companionship.

They also recognize that the marriage bond is sacred. It is a gift from God and a covenant. It is not to be violated by adultery. Thus they work hard at rejecting the sinful temptations offered by the society around them.

In 1 Samuel 1:8, Hannah's husband, Elkanah, makes an interesting statement: "Don't I mean more to you than ten sons?" We usually interpret this as insensitivity on Elkanah's part. He did not understand Hannah's hurt. It can also be interpreted as a perceptive insight: "Our intimate marriage relationship with one another as husband and wife should be more important than having children." He was right. The covenant that husband and wife have with one another is like no other relationship in the world.

The sages implored husbands to give their complete attention to their wives. This requires constant and firm mental and emotional discipline (Prov. 5:11-13, 21-23). The sages were aware that some women were seductive and adulterous. They called these women "strange" or "foreign" (zār or nokrî; 2:16, NASB), meaning they were unrelated to the husband. They were also immoral. They had left their first husband and were seeking liaisons with other men (vv. 16-19). Over sixty-five verses in Proverbs warn men to stay away from such women. If men turn to them and away from their wives, it will lead to the loss of their reputation (5:9), the loss of their wealth (v. 10), the loss of their health (v. 11), and the loss of their freedom (v. 22). It may even lead to physical confrontation with the husband of the adulterous woman (6:32-35) and death (2:16-19; 5:5). So why would a man want to do that? The rhetorical questions that the sages proposed are powerful:

Can a man scoop fire into his lap
> without his clothes being burned?
Can a man walk on hot coals
> without his feet being scorched?
So is he who sleeps with another man's wife;
> no one who touches her will go unpunished. (6:27-29)

With these cleverly worded questions, the sages tried to place a flashing red light in front of all young men. According to verses 26-33, the consequences of adultery are severe. They are also inevitable and unending. We are tempted to deceive ourselves into thinking that we can do sinful things in secret and get away with them. But that is not the case. God is aware of everything, including adultery (5:21). We cannot hide our sins from him.

Adultery is also an affront against society. It attacks the stability of our homes and the health of our communities because it is based on secrecy, lies, betrayal, and distrust. What kinds of lessons do children learn from parents who are fooling around with other partners? What kind of community is created when people are trying to destroy relationships rather than build them up? Most societies have laws against adultery because it is an insidious attack against the family and community and it deserves punishment.

The sages directed their exhortations on adultery primarily to young men, suggesting that women were the ones on the prowl. However, their words apply equally to both men and women in today's world. Whether you are a husband or wife, reject immediately any temptations from adulterous-minded people. Adultery will destroy you, your marriage, and every good thing in your life if you don't. The sages labeled adulterers as fools; they have no sense (v. 23; 6:32). Why would you want to associate with fools?

The key to avoiding adultery is discipline. In their exhortations on adultery, the sages stressed this thought multiple times (4:23, 26-27; 5:11-13, 22-23; 6:23). So what is your level of discipline right now? Is it strong, or are you struggling with temptation? Do you feel you are trapped in the undisciplined, moral mindset of the world (5:22)? Good marriage partners recognize that discipline is needed to keep one's attention where it ought to be. Moreover, God can help us do that if we will make him the third partner in our marriage.

Possible Sermon Titles: "Characteristics of a Good Marriage," "How's Your Marriage Going?" "Need a Marriage Tune-up?" "Flashing Red Lights Concerning Marriage," "He Who Finds a Wife Finds What Is Good," "A Good Spouse Is a Gift from God"

What's in a Name? (Prov. 22:1)

Proverbs 22:1 is a one-verse text that can be easily crafted into a sermon using other verses in Proverbs to provide a larger context:

A good name is to be chosen rather than great riches,
    and favor is better than silver or gold. (NRSV)

It is a typical "better-than" proverb that makes a comparison between two items. There are twenty-two of these in Proverbs (3:14; 8:11, 19; 12:9; 15:16-17; 16:8, 16, 19, 32; 17:1, 12; 19:1, 22; 21:9, 19; 22:1; 25:7, 24; 27:5, 10; 28:6). There are another twenty-seven in Psalms, Ecclesiastes, and the Song of Songs.

Some other "better than" proverbs are scattered here and there throughout the rest of the OT. One of the most well known in the narrative literature is Samuel's words to King Saul: "To obey is better than sacrifice, and to heed is better than the fat of rams" (1 Sam. 15:22b). Some examples of Jesus's usage of this form are found in Matthew 18:6-9. Paul uses the same form in 1 Corinthians 7:9. A modern English example of this type of proverb is "Better late than never."

What all these examples imply is that there are choices to be made in life. Some choices are inconsequential, such as choosing a breakfast cereal in the morning or clothes to wear for the day. However, other choices are crucially important for the quality of our lives on earth. They may even affect our eternal destiny. These latter choices are the kind that the writers of "better than" proverbs attempt to address.

When using Proverbs 22:1 for preaching or teaching, preachers should select a translation that emphasizes the importance of *choosing* the better option. The NIV does not do this. It simply makes a statement that one option "is more desirable" than the other. Nothing is said about choosing the better one. The impression is given that readers should think about whether they want to be known as a good person or a wealthy person, but no challenge is given to make the better choice. In contrast, the NRSV not only stresses that one option is of more value but also encourages readers to choose the more valuable one. The verb "choose" (*bḥr*) is found in the Hebrew text, so that needs to be included in the translation.

The meaning of this proverb is not hard to figure out: a good reputation is of much more value than wealth, and we should pursue that goal in life. The author is not saying that wealth is bad, for it is one of the gifts that Lady Wisdom is able to provide her followers (3:16; 8:18). The author is merely stating that some things in life are more valuable than others. We should choose those goals in life that are the most valuable.

However, this proverb is only a single verse. It needs additional scriptural support to answer some of our questions that are not addressed. Here is where we need to mine the book of Proverbs for other passages that amplify the basic meaning. We examine these using three questions.

First, are there any other verses in Proverbs that support this theme or add further clarity to its meaning? The answer is yes. Several comparative proverbs place other pursuits in life ahead of wealth if one has to make a choice. They include the "fear of the LORD" (15:16), "righteousness" (16:8), "wisdom" and understanding (v. 16), "knowledge" (20:15), and integrity (28:6). This collection of verses makes it clear that wealth should never be a primary goal in life. There are so many more worthy endeavors to pursue.

Second, why is wealth not a high goal in life? Here are several verses that attempt to answer that question. Wealth has no lasting value (10:2; 11:28). It can quickly vanish (23:4-5; 28:22). It will lead to trouble (28:20). It has no value in turbulent times (11:4). People sometimes resort to dishonest, illegal, wicked, or violent ways of obtaining it (v. 16; 21:6; 28:20, 22).

Third, what is so valuable about a good reputation that would place its worth above wealth? Proverbs 10:7 helps to answer that question:

The memory of the righteous is a blessing,

but the name of the wicked will rot. (NRSV)

Wealth is tangible—we can see and touch it. Thus it is more attractive to people than an intangible quality, like a good reputation. Nevertheless, we cannot take wealth with us into the afterlife (27:23-24). As Ecclesiastes 2:18-19 notes, who knows what the people who inherit our wealth will do with it after we are gone? The goods and money we have worked so hard for in life could be squandered on meaningless, selfish pursuits. In contrast, a good reputation not only brings blessings now but also will outlive us by many years. Family and friends will remember our good deeds for generations. Jesus echoed this criticism of pursuing wealth over other goals in life in his parable of the rich man (Luke 12:15-21).

The proverbs above place wealth in a comparative position to other priorities in life. The point is that wealth is not as valuable as many people think it is. We should think carefully when setting goals in life. God needs to be consulted for this, for only he has the wisdom needed to make long-range plans that will result in a good reputation.

Let us apply this verse to our own lives today with some comments about the meaning of "a good name" (Prov. 22:1). Each of us has a name that was given to us at birth by our parents. It is a term that identifies us and separates us from everyone else in the world. When we hear our name spoken, we prick up our ears—we pay close attention because we know that someone is speaking to or about us.

Some parents go to great lengths to create an elaborate, original name. For example, how would you like to have this name: Charles Philip Arthur George, Prince of Wales, Earl of Chester, Duke of Cornwall, Duke of Rothesay, Earl of Carrick, Baron of Renfrew, Lord of the Isles, Prince and Great Steward of Scotland, and Heir to the throne of the United Kingdom? How would you like to have to sign that name on all your checks? That is why he was better known as Prince Charles, now King Charles III.

Other names are rather short. There was an entertainer a few years back who went by the name of Mr. T and a basketball player known as Dr. J.

Some people like their names. Others detest what their parents chose for them. Hence, they go by a nickname, or use only their initials. Some years back there was a man running for President of the United States whose name was Gary Hart. The media investigated his life and soon found out that he was born Gary Hartpence. But he did not like that name, so he changed it to Gary Hart.

How many people would have chosen the names they have if they had been allowed to choose? What would you have named yourself? The fact is, you were not given a choice. It was already decided for you before you could even pronounce your name. There are some who found out later that they were stuck with an old family heirloom that had been around for generations. The name most people know me by is Wendell Bowes. But Wendell is not my first name; it is actually Alpin. That was my father's name and my grandfather's name and my great-grandfather's name. Fortunately, my wife and I only had girls, so we were not obligated to pass that name on to our children. They are very grateful for that.

According to Proverbs 22:1, a good name is an important asset in life. This is not about the sound of the name. It is an achievable goal in life that we have to choose and work toward gaining. Let me suggest three thoughts that you should keep in mind as you carry your name through life.

1. Your Name Represents Your Parents' Dreams

Almost four decades ago, I undertook a massive project of studying people's names—people who lived in what we call the Old Babylonian period, that is, the time of Abraham (ca. 2000–1500 BC). I collected over fifteen thousand of these Old Babylonian names while working on my doctoral dissertation.

In the process of that research, it was easy to get lost in the statistics and forget that every name represented a precious baby to some young couple. At times, one can almost see the smile on their faces as they gave a name to a new child: *Nidnī* (My gift) or *Ilī-iddinam* (My god has given to me). *Ummī-waqrat* (My mother is precious) may have been given to a child who was born on an ancient Mother's Day. Other times, one can easily visualize a frown, a sense of disappointment, or an expression of fear: *Ātanah-ilī* (I am weary, O my god), *Sēret-ilīya* (The punishment of my god), *Maṣi-ilī* (Enough, O god).

However, whatever the name (whether positive or negative), a name represents the parents' best efforts to start that child on a good path in life. Parents want the best for their children. Choosing the right name is one way parents express their hopes for the future of each child.

Biblical names were often chosen because of some event at the time of birth, out of thankfulness to God for giving a child, or to emphasize a parent's hopes for that child. For example, "Samuel" means "Heard of God," "Isaac" means "He laughs," "Ishmael" means "God hears," "Jacob" means "He grasps the heel," and "Benjamin" means "Son of my right hand." All of these names were chosen because they signified something important to the parents at the time of birth.

The naming of children is an important assignment in life, and many parents have a hard time making that decision. The debate may go on for nine months. As the date of birth gets closer and closer, the anxiety increases because as parents we know we are about to do

III. INDIVIDUAL SAYINGS ATTRIBUTED TO SOLOMON

something permanent that will mark this newborn child for the rest of his or her life. "Shall I name my child after myself? Shall I call him Junior? Or will he later resent that?" "Shall I name her after her grandmother? Or will the other grandmother resent that?" "Shall I choose a Bible name? Or an old family name? Or a modern name?" "Does it matter what the name means?" "What nickname will the kids at school make out of this name?" "What do the initials stand for?"

Whatever name your parents gave to you, it represents their hopes and dreams for you. They were so proud when you were born, and the name they gave you is one they liked. If you have not already done so, you ought to ask your parents sometime about how they chose your name and what they envisioned for you as you were growing up. It might surprise you what was going through their thinking.

2. Your Name Represents a Personality

At every college in the United States, there are probably thirty or more students named Timothy. There are probably the same number named Robert or Anna or Rachel. But when we hear that name and attach a last name to it, immediately we have an image of a unique personality named Timothy or Robert or Anna or Rachel. The reason is that each person has taken the name given by his or her parents at birth and has filled it full of meaning.

"Robert" is no longer just a Teutonic term meaning "Of shining fame." "Robert" is no longer just an old family name that has been in the family for generations. No, "Robert" now stands for a six-foot-tall, nineteen-year-old sophomore with brown hair and blue eyes. He is somewhat introverted and has a hard time asking a girl for a date. He likes sports but is not good enough to try out for a team. He likes college but makes average grades because he does not always do his homework. The point is that there may be thirty people on a college campus named Robert. Each one of them has filled that name with a different meaning. Every Robert is unique. What your personality is, is far more important than the actual words of your name.

The same is true in the business world. When you go for a job interview, your future employer is not interested in what your name is, what it means, or whether it is an old family heirloom. All the interviewer wants to know is the personality and skills your name represents. Can you work with people? What is your attitude toward authority? Can you contribute to our company? That is something you cannot hide behind a name or a style of dress or the way you comb your hair. It is something you have been forming for years and years. Moreover, you are about to see whether you have formed it well or not.

The point of Proverbs 22:1 is not that we should change our name if we do not like it. Rather, we should strive to attach a good reputation to our name. Any name, no matter how strange it sounds, can become a source of inspiration and blessing to others if we make good choices in life. The book of Proverbs encourages us to seek after the best things in life, things that are pleasing to God and have long-lasting benefit, such as the fear of the Lord, righteousness, and wisdom.

How would you like to have a name like Engelbert Humperdinck? That is not his real name, but imagine if it were. Can you imagine what kids would call you out on the playground? Yet this man has taken this strange-sounding name and made millions of dollars off it by filling it with beautiful music. We can do something similar with our own names.

3. Your Name Represents a Deity

In my study of Old Babylonian names, I found this to be true. The majority of names in Abraham's time included their deity's name right in their personal name. For example, *Šamaš-abī* (Shamash is my father), *Šamaš-nāṣirī* (Shamash is my protector), *Anum-mušēzibī* (Anum is my savior), *Anum-muballiṭ* (Anum is the life giver), *Ištar-emūqī* (Ishtar is my strength), *Ištar-ummī* (Ishtar is my mother). Similarly, Hebrew names often included the name of their God in them as well. "Samuel," "Ishmael," and "Israel" are names that contain God's name in them.

Shamash was the Babylonian sun god, Anum was the high god in the pantheon, and Ishtar was the mother goddess.

The more I studied ancient names, the more I came to realize that each of *our* names represents a deity as well. Our individual names may not actually contain God's name, but everyone who knows us knows exactly who our deity is and knows about our relationship to him. They see our God in our attitude toward religious things such as the church and the Bible. They see our God in our attitude toward money and the way we spend it. They see our God in the way we treat other people. They see our God in the way we respond to criticism. They see our God in the places we go and the things we do. In short, everything we do and say is a reflection not only of our individual personalities but also of our relationship with our deity.

It does not matter what our name is. It could be a biblical name such as Jesus or Mary. The fact of the matter is that we cannot hide the deity we serve. It is obvious to everyone.

You may not like your name, the family you grew up in, or the environment in which you were raised. That is all right. God understands that. He knows you did not choose those things. Even so, God does hold us accountable for what we have done with our name, for what personality we have attached to it, and for what deity we have chosen to serve. Those are matters of crucial significance.

There were many people named Jesus in the first century AD, and there have been many more since. However, the one we remember the most is the one who died on a Roman cross and rose from the dead on the third day. He made his name beautiful by what he did with that name. We, too, can add beauty to our name.

Possible Sermon Titles: "What Is Your Name?" "What Does Your Name Represent?" "Do You Like Your Name?" "Names That Mean Something"

Advice for Parents (Prov. 22:6)

The sages of Israel had studied parent-child relationships over many centuries. Their observations led them to believe that successful homes were usually guided by some key principles that brought order to them. These principles are expressed in over 160 sayings in the book of Proverbs. Therefore, preachers and teachers have many resources to guide their comments. The sayings are directed at two groups—parents and children. Only about a dozen deal with recommendations for parents. The rest provide advice for children. If followed, they will help children grow up to fear God and become wise and mature people. In an earlier sermon we examined what advice

Proverbs has for children (→ "Advice for Children," p. 85). In this sermon, we will look at what Proverbs says to parents. Before we begin, there are two cautions that need to be kept in mind.

First, as was mentioned in the introduction, these proverbs are not presented as guarantees that every child will turn out well if the principles are put into practice. Every child has a free will, and more than one saying acknowledges that children can bring grief to their parents (10:1; 11:29; 15:20; 17:21, 25; 19:13). However, the sages believed that if their principles were put into practice in the home, more likely than not, the children in these families would make their parents proud.

Second, the background for all proverbs is the most common family setting—a father, a mother, and at least one child. There is no discussion of other family arrangements, such as single parents, grandparents serving as parents, siblings serving as parents, and gay or lesbian parents. Such topics would need further amplification in a modern setting, but the overall principles would remain the same.

1. Fear the Lord

> Whoever fears the LORD has a secure fortress,
>> and for their children it will be a refuge. (Prov. 14:26)

To make the right impact on their children, parents must begin with themselves. They must develop a wisdom about life that places God at the center of everything. The OT describes this as fearing the Lord. According to the earlier sermon "How to Be Successful and Wise" (ch. 1, p. 27), the fear of the Lord means to hold God in awe and reverence, to submit one's life to him, and to behave in a manner that reflects one's relationship to God as Lord and Savior. The fear of the Lord is the undergirding theme for the entire book of Proverbs (1:7), so it is no surprise that parents are urged to establish a relationship with God and model righteous behavior in their own lives. If they do so, their children will have a proper example to learn from and follow.

Proverbs 14:26 suggests that parents who fear the Lord have a strong confidence that God will provide security and protection amid life's troubles. For them, God is "a secure fortress" and "a refuge." Their confidence is not in themselves or other people. It derives from their knowledge that they can always draw upon God's love and strength through any situation in life. Children who grow up in that kind of atmosphere experience God's security and protection resulting from their parents' godly lives. This teaches them to trust in the same God as their parents. They start to make the connection between serving God and living a blessed life (20:7).

2. Train Your Children

> Start children off on the way they should go,
>> and even when they are old they will not turn from it. (Prov. 22:6)

Children do not grow up well by themselves. They need the nurturing of good parents—parents who will patiently instruct them, encourage them when they make mistakes, and model the kind of life that God wants them to live. Proverbs 22:6 presents this as an admonition that God expects of all parents. The reason for this training is that children left to themselves will bring disgrace and grief on their family (10:1; 11:29; 15:20; 17:21, 25; 19:13). Children have to be molded and shaped and pointed down the right pathway.

This principle does not always hold true in the animal kingdom. Some species have no parental responsibility at all. They merely lay their eggs and leave the hatchlings to figure out life on their own, with only the assistance of instinct. In contrast, human beings need about eighteen years to prepare their children for life.

I asked a man one day if he would let his children ride our church bus to Sunday school. His response was, "I'm going to let my children decide for themselves whether they want to go to church." In effect, he was saying, "I wash my hands of any responsibility for the spiritual welfare of my children." My guess is his children never darkened the door of any church, because they saw it was unimportant to their father.

Instruction is an important part of training. This is emphasized repeatedly in Proverbs using the term "my son" (e.g., 2:1-5; 3:1-2; 7:1-4). Proverbs 3 and 4 contain some of the best verses in the book on the types of instructions that parents should be teaching their children. The primary topic, of course, is wisdom and the benefits that derive from seeking and finding it (3:13-18, 21-22; 4:5-11) (→ earlier sermon "Wisdom's Rewards," p. 51). Other topics include trusting in God (3:5-

6); avoiding evil, wickedness, and violence (vv. 7-8, 31; 4:14-17, 19, 26-27); honoring God with a portion of your income (3:9-10); accepting God's discipline (vv. 11-12); and treating your neighbor with kindness (vv. 27-30).

What is fascinating in Proverbs about the parents' instructions to their children is that they are the same instructions they received from their own parents and likely from their grandparents, great-grandparents, and so on before them (4:3-5). In other words, each generation does not have to create a new curriculum for their children. The basic principles of child-rearing in a godly setting have remained the same for hundreds of years because they have been proven true time and time again. This should encourage parents that they are following tried-and-true methods of training their children for adulthood.

Perhaps the most important point here is the absolute necessity of parents creating an order for their children's lives that draws upon the wisdom of the ages and has biblical support. Parents need to ask themselves, "Are we 'pass[ing] on a heritage of wisdom to our children or simply cav[ing] in to what we see and hear in the surrounding culture'?" (Treier 2011, 32).

3. Discipline Your Children

Discipline your children, for in that there is hope;
> do not be a willing party to their death. (Prov. 19:18)

Discipline your children, and they will give you peace;
> they will bring you the delights you desire. (29:17)

A rod and a reprimand impart wisdom,
> but a child left undisciplined disgraces its mother. (v. 15)

Discipline in the home refers to bringing order into people's lives. It includes both instructions in the ways of life and corrections or punishments for misdeeds. There are seven passages in Proverbs that refer to discipline in the home, so this was an important topic in the minds of the sages. Children are not born with order in their lives (22:15). They need to be disciplined by diligent, loving parents. This discipline is especially important in the early years of childhood, before children become set in their ways (19:18).

The sages had discovered that a lack of parental discipline led to a child's death (v. 18; 23:13-14). By that, they meant that children left to their own devices would likely follow a pathway that led to their early destruction. "If you do not desire your son's death, you will punish his wrongdoings, so that he not continue on the deadly path of folly" (Fox 2009, 657).

The method of discipline preferred by the sages was spanking with a rod (10:13; 13:24; 19:29; 20:30; 22:15; 23:13-14; 26:3). They also recommended verbal reproofs ("reprimand" [29:15]). Obviously, times have changed. Psychologists and family counselors have given modern parents many other ways to discipline their children without harming them physically. New parents should read some books on child discipline and then discuss with each other the methods they plan to use in their own family. The method you choose is probably not as important as the fact that you have a plan and you are consistent in its application. The point is that wishy-washy parents turn out confused kids. The hope is that parental discipline in the home will lead to self-discipline when the children depart.

We need to remember, though, that no discipline plan works 100 percent of the time. Every child has a free will. Some choose to rebel or live a life of laziness or even curse or rob their parents (19:26; 28:24; 30:11, 17). More likely than not, however, if parents follow the principles of the sages, their children will grow up to make them proud.

4. Leave an Inheritance

> A good person leaves an inheritance for their children's children, but a sinner's wealth is stored up for the righteous. (Prov. 13:22)

Inheritances in ancient times primarily consisted of land, houses or tents, and animals. Today's inheritances usually lack animals (unless one is a farmer), but they include other monetary valuables, such as the proceeds of insurance policies, annuities, and trusts. However, the intent of an inheritance remains the same today—to pass on to our children and grandchildren the wealth we have accumulated over our lifetimes. The thought that goes through most parents' minds is, "I want my children and grandchildren to be better off than I am."

According to Proverbs 13:22, this transfer of wealth from one generation to the next occurs smoothly and profitably in homes where the parents are "good"—that is, they fear the Lord and teach their children to do the same. However, the proverb goes on to point out the tragedy that befalls parents who are sinners. Likely, their wealth was gained through devious means and greed. Then, when it is passed on to the next generation, the children, who have not been trained or disciplined, squander it away to others. The point is that if parents want their inheritance to endure, they had better live a righteous life themselves and pass those principles along to their children, in addition to whatever wealth they have accumulated. Job 27:13-17 also speaks of the loss of inheritance by the children of the wicked.

Granted, many people do not have a monetary inheritance to pass on to their children. They have spent their last years in a nursing home without a house, a car, a life insurance policy, or a bank account. However, one's heritage includes much more than financial wealth. Things such as (1) a strong faith in God, (2) a disciplined life, (3) a happy disposition, (4) a caring attitude, (5) a wise mind that is full of good advice, (6) a lifetime of good memories, and (7) an album full of family photos are probably worth far more to a grieving family than a large bank account. In fact, those types of inheritances endure for longer than a windfall of wealth. As Proverbs 1:8-9 notes,

Listen, my son, to your father's instruction
and do not forsake your mother's teaching.
They are a garland to grace your head
and a chain to adorn your neck.

I have conducted numerous funerals in which it was my privilege to recount the legacy of a godly saint, whose life was lacking in money but well lived.

In addition, one other thought is worth keeping in mind. People do not have to wait until they die to give away an inheritance to the next generation. An inheritance of "faith, hope and love" can be given away every day (1 Cor. 13:13; see vv. 1-13).

5. Make Your Children Proud

Children's children are a crown to the aged,
and parents are the pride of their children. (Prov. 17:6)

To have a fool for a child brings grief;
> there is no joy for the parent of a godless fool. (v. 21)

Two thoughts occupy these verses. The first is the importance of healthy mutual pride among the members of a family. One has only to listen to a mother talk about her children for a few minutes to know whether she is proud of her children or not. Proud mothers love to show pictures too! Nevertheless, pride does not develop naturally. It has to be nurtured. Parents have to take the first step by investing in their children's growth and development, by loving them continually, and by speaking about them with pride. By doing so, they teach their children that they deeply love and care for them. This, then, creates the atmosphere for children to love in return. This love may not be as evident during the teen years, when children are trying to establish their own identities. Then, when they become adults, they will "come to realize that their station in life comes from the efforts of their parents" (Hartley 2016, 190). They will appreciate how much their parents loved and sacrificed for them. This realization will create a sense of gratitude and pride that they grew up in your family. They will say, "I am so proud that I am a Bowes (or whatever your family name is)!"

Proverbs 23:24-25 speaks of the joy and delight that come to parents when their children grow up to be godly and wise. Usually, the feeling is mutual. Good children and grandchildren speak of their parents and grandparents with love, respect, and pride.

However, the second thought is that where sin has entered the home, parents and/or children are living foolish lives. There is grief rather than joy according to Proverbs 17:21 (also 10:1; 17:25). They will probably experience the breakup of their family and its impoverishment (11:29). "Godless families collapse . . . and godless children bring their parents shame" (Waltke 2005, 42).

One other topic that could be discussed at the conclusion of this sermon is how grandparents fit into the picture. Most congregations are blessed with a good number of grandparents. Generally, grandparents do not have younger children in their home, so a lesson on parent-child relationships seems irrelevant. Actually, the opposite is the case. Here are three areas where the influence of grandparents can benefit both children and grandchildren.

(1) Grandparents, continue to fear the Lord and practice your own self-discipline. Just because your kids are no longer living under your roof does not free you to throw aside the principles you practiced when you were younger. Grown kids do watch their parents. They will admire your self-discipline and be reminded of its importance in their own lives. It may spur them to be more disciplined themselves.

(2) When your grandchildren are under your care, treat them as responsibly as you would your own kids. You are not helping your children teach discipline if you are spoiling your grandkids. Before you babysit, find out from your children what their discipline plan is and then stick to it.

(3) If you are given the opportunity to work with children in a Sunday school class, vacation Bible school, a camp, or scouting, don't let the kids run over you. Establish your discipline plan at the beginning of the encounter and then carry through with it.

Possible Sermon Titles: "Children That Will Make You Proud," "An Investment in the Next Generation," "Train Up a Child," "Make Your Children Proud," "Parent-Child Relationships," "Guidelines for Parents"

IV. THIRTY "SAYINGS OF THE WISE" (PROV. 22:17–24:22)

Old Testament scholars have noted the similarity of this division of Proverbs (consisting of thirty sayings of one or more verses each) to an Egyptian wisdom writing from about the time of Solomon. In 1922-24, British archaeologist Wallis Budge published some articles comparing Proverbs 22:17–24:22 to the *Instruction of Amenemope* in Egypt. Both writings have thirty sayings and discuss some of the same topics. In addition, the *Instruction of Amenemope* has some similar wording to Psalm 1 and Jeremiah 17:5-8. Thus this passage has received a great deal of discussion in scholarly circles. Scholars debate whether one author copied from the other or whether both authors borrowed from a lost third source.

Some of the topics in Proverbs 22:17–24:22 include warnings against exploiting the poor (saying 2), proper etiquette when dining with a ruler or begrudging host (sayings 7, 9), warnings against associating with fools and the wicked (sayings 10, 20), encouragement to parents to discipline their children (saying 13), encouragement to children to obey their parents (saying 17), the dangers of drinking wine (sayings 16, 19), and the importance of striving after wisdom and fearing the Lord (sayings 12, 14, 15, 21, 26). The sermon we develop from this division of Proverbs is based on sayings 5 (22:28) and 11 (23:10-11).

Don't Move Those Stones! (Prov. 22:28; 23:10-11)

When the Israelites under Joshua's leadership settled in the land of Canaan, they put into effect a plan to divide the land (Josh. 13–21). Each tribe was assigned a general area. The tribal leaders further divided the land into subdivisions for each clan and finally for each family within a clan. As new generations came along, the land was again divided among sons and grandsons until some plots were quite small. Always, families understood that this land was theirs forever.

It was the task of each family to prepare their land for farming. In some cases, the land had already been cultivated by its previous owners—the Canaanites. In other cases, the plots needed considerable work to prepare them for cultivation. This meant cutting down trees, pulling up or burning away grass and bushes, and removing thousands of stones that are common in Israelite soil. Usually the stones were placed at the edges of the property and used for fences and boundary stones. These boundary stones are the subject of the verses in our text.

> Do not move an ancient boundary stone
>> set up by your ancestors. (Prov. 22:28)

> Do not move an ancient boundary stone
>> or encroach on the fields of the fatherless,
> for their Defender is strong;
>> he will take up their case against you. (23:10-11)

These passages warn against moving another family's boundary stones. To do so would be stealing another family's property by diminishing the amount of land that family had to support itself. Even more significantly, it meant stealing an inheritance that could be traced back for centuries to the time of Joshua. Each plot of ground was considered a sacred gift God had given to a particular family. Israelite law protected it (Gen. 13:14-17; 15:18-21; Exod. 23:31; Deut. 19:14; 27:17; Josh. 13:8–19:51; 24:13). Further, Leviticus 25:23 makes clear that the entire land of Israel actually belonged to God. The Israelites were just tenants, allowed by God to till the ground and produce food for their needs. The story of the conflict between King Ahab and Naboth over a vineyard Naboth owned illustrates how seriously the Israelites felt about maintaining a family's property inheritance (1 Kings 21:1-3).

Human beings have regarded stealing in any form as a crime since the beginning of written law codes. The *Reforms of Urukagina* (twenty-fourth c. BC) and the magnificent *Code of Hammurabi* (eighteenth to seventeenth c. BC) are two examples of ANE law codes that condemn such kinds of stealing. Most law codes stated the circumstances of the offense and the punishment to be imposed on the criminal. Scholars call this format *casuistic* law (e.g., see the *Code of Hammurabi*, nos. 8-14, 22-23 [*ANET*, 166-67]). The law against stealing in the Ten Commandments is very different. It merely states a broad prohibition against stealing, without circumstances or penalty: "You shall not steal" (Exod. 20:15). This is called *apodictic* law—an absolute prohibition under any and all circumstances. Other places in the OT describe specific forms of stealing and the associated penalties. According to OT law, there are at least eight general categories of possessions that should not be stolen:

- Animals (Exod. 22:1-4)
- Grain (vv. 5-6)
- Money (lit., silver or items of exchange used for buying and selling) (vv. 7-8)
- Clothing (v. 9)
- The wages that rightfully belong to an employer's workers (Lev. 19:13)
- Property (Deut. 19:14)
- People—that is, kidnapping (24:7)
- Tithes and offerings (Mal. 3:8-9)

In addition, there are numerous admonitions dealing with wrongful treatment of the poor that could be classified as stealing their rightful livelihood (e.g., Deut. 15:7-11; Job 24:2-4, 9; Isa. 10:1-4; Zech. 7:10).

The corresponding penalties for these crimes included such things as fines, restitution, curses, and even death (in the case of kidnapping). If preachers and teachers feel a need to present some personal stories to illustrate the consequences that went with various types of stealing, they could mention the stories of Jacob (Gen. 27:30-36, 41-45; 29:15-28), Joseph (40:14-15), Achan (Josh. 6:18-21; 7:1, 16-26), and the conflict between the rich and the poor in Nehemiah's day (Neh. 5:1-13). In the NT, Jesus encountered a tax collector named Zacchaeus (Luke 19:1-10). Most assume he had probably defrauded numerous people. He was so grateful for Jesus's willingness to come to his house that he offered to refund four times any money he may have stolen through his work. He was serious about getting right with God.

The crime of moving boundary stones was probably fairly easy to carry out if the owners were away from their property for a time. It would be difficult for the rightful owners to prove that a crime had been committed without standardized plot plans and surveyors' measurements that we store in municipal records today.

The crime was especially insidious when perpetrated against the fields of widows and orphans. People who had no adult male figure in their families were especially vulnerable to predatory individuals who might take advantage of their low status and relocate the boundary stones of their property. Widows and orphans probably would not have had the resources needed to go to court to retrieve their land, and so they might have to sell themselves to another landholder as slaves. As a result, special instructions were given in Israelite law to protect widows and orphans (Deut. 24:17-22). Proverbs goes even further by stating that God will defend vulnerable widows and orphans and bring punishment against property snatchers (Prov. 15:25; 23:10-11).

This proverb on boundary stones is also mentioned in the *Instruction of Amenemope* (no. 6, 7:12–9:8; *AEL*, vol. 2, 151-52; Fox 2009, 731-32). This implies that illegally moving boundary stones was a problem in both Egypt and Israel.

Stealing land by moving boundary markers is not a common problem in modern Western society. However, it does open up the topic of stealing in general. The Bible is clear that taking something that belongs to another is a sin that God detests and will judge. In fact, according to Paul, thieves and swindlers will be excluded from the kingdom of God (1 Cor. 6:9-10).

Thieves today have dreamed up many more ways of stealing. Here are some examples:

- Shoplifting
- Ponzi schemes
- Stealing from the government by not reporting income on one's taxes
- Stealing from employers by snitching products, taking long breaks, failing to give a full day's work for a full day's wage
- Stealing from employees by failing to pay a decent wage while taking an enormous salary as CEO

- Stealing from an insurance company by claiming excessive damages on an item of furniture worth far less
- Choosing to go into debt beyond a reasonable amount and then declaring bankruptcy
- Taking money from the household budget and spending it on gambling and lotteries
- Putting inferior products in a house or building that you are constructing for a client

One especially troublesome form is the stealing made possible through the internet—plagiarism, stealing another's intellectual property, stealing a person's identity, stealing from another's bank account by hacking, and shutting down another's computer files by means of ransomware. Both companies and individuals have been severely harmed through internet stealing. In addition, a great deal of character stealing takes place today in newspaper tabloids, on radio and TV talk shows, and through political name-calling. None of this is pleasing to God.

The excuses to justify these modern kinds of stealing are numerous:

- The government is corrupt, and politicians are getting rich off of us.
- This is a big store, bank, or insurance company that makes lots of money. They will not miss it.
- Everyone else is doing it.
- I've been ripped off by others, so now it's my turn.
- I need this more than they do.

Stealing, today, is a huge problem. Millions of dollars are pilfered every day. It is a reflection of the fact that many people in this world have twisted values. They have never surrendered their lives to Christ or attempted to live by the Golden Rule. Hopefully, some will become convicted and repent of their sinful ways. Here is what thieves need to do:

1. Seek God's Forgiveness (1 John 1:9)

When we break a biblical commandment, we become sinners in the eyes of God. We should experience guilt. The only way to deal with guilt is to confess our sins to God. He alone can give us a clean heart. He will do so, if we acknowledge that we are thieves.

2. Make Restitution with the Wronged Person(s) (Ezek. 33:14-16)

Thieves need to make right whatever wrongs have been committed. Jesus did not even have to tell Zacchaeus to refund the money he had taken wrongly from other people. He knew instinctively that if he was going to be a follower of Jesus, he had to make restitution (Luke 19:8).

3. Those Who Steal because of Poverty Should Ask God to Help Them Find a Way Out of Poverty (Eph. 4:28)

Paul admonished the Ephesians to quit stealing to support themselves and get a job instead. This is good advice in many situations, but we also know that this is often easier said than done. Some people have great difficulty in finding a job that pays enough to live on. There are medical issues, personal and family issues, social issues, racial issues, and economic issues (e.g., recessions and inflation) that can make it almost impossible to find work.

Sometimes God and Christian friends may be able to open doors that lead to suitable employment. Many Christians have discovered ways to help people in these situations by contributing money and time to organizations that help the needy, such as rescue missions, welfare agencies, food banks, and so on. Sometimes our greatest contribution can be in voting for would-be political leaders who really care about the poor and promote policies that lift people out of poverty.

4. Cultivate a Life of Devotion to God and Resist Greed and Materialism (1 Tim. 6:10)

Many cultures today are self-centered and consumerist, valuing what one has more than who one is. Christians constantly have to do battle with advertising that promotes the idea that we must own a certain car or smartphone or item of clothing in order to be successful. We desperately need to develop a healthy biblical understanding of the meaning of possessions. Job wisely observed that our possessions do not really belong to us. They belong to God. He graciously loans them to us for a period, but he may recall them at any time:

The LORD gave and the LORD has taken away;
> may the name of the LORD be praised. (Job 1:21)

We must learn to appreciate and use God's gifts appropriately in our service to him, while at the same time learning to hold them lightly, for he may take them back when he desires to do so.

In 2012, our house was broken into and burglarized while we were on vacation. The thieves were apparently only interested in metal objects they could easily pawn or melt down, for they made off with all my wife's jewelry and the few silver dishes we owned. None of her jewelry was worth much, but a couple items had a great deal of sentimental value. I was terribly angry at the burglars for having taken some irreplaceable items I had given to my wife on special occasions. Sometime later, I finally accepted that all our possessions really belong to God. We had enjoyed them while we had them, but we would go on without them. There are far more important things in life than jewelry.

One way to expand this sermon would be to mention other rules in life that are just as inviolable as this one on moving boundary stones. The Ten Commandments would be a good place to begin (Exod. 20:1-17). In the NT, Jesus's teachings on the two greatest commandments would be another important passage (Matt. 22:34-39). The important point to leave with your congregation is that God has tried to create order in human life by presenting specific rules to live by. Those who live by these rules are wise, and they will reap the benefits God provides for his followers. Those who reject God's order are fools. Their lives will be pitiful and meaningless, both in this life and in the next.

Possible Sermon Titles: "No Stealing!" "Stones That Should Never Be Moved," "Rules That Should Never Be Broken"

V. ADDITIONAL "SAYINGS OF THE WISE" (PROV. 24:23-34)

This brief collection of twelve verses is titled "Additional 'Sayings of the Wise.'" The relationship of these sayings to the previous divisions is unknown. There are five main topics: (1) the need for judicial proceedings to be conducted impartially, (2) the importance of honesty, (3) the need to organize one's activities and prioritize the most important, (4) some suggestions on maintaining good relations with neighbors, and (5) the consequences of laziness. The sermon starter from this section focuses on the last topic—laziness. This might be a good sermon to preach on Labor Day Sunday.

Laziness (Prov. 24:30–34)

The book of Proverbs has many negative things to say about three categories of people who are outside of God's kingdom for moral reasons—simple people, fools, and mockers (→ earlier sermon "Not All Fools Are the Same," p. 46). The latter two categories could even be characterized as antagonistic to God and his people. But there is a fourth type of person that Proverbs also criticizes frequently—sluggards. These people have a major character flaw that makes them useless to God.

The Hebrew word attached to this person is *'āṣēl*. It refers to one who is slow or sluggish. Their slowness is not due to a disability or medical condition. It is totally a personal choice about how to live one's life. English versions usually translate the word as "sluggard," "lazy person," or "lazybones." There are sixteen references to the sluggard in Proverbs (6:6, 9; 10:26; 13:4; 15:19; 19:15, 24; 20:4; 21:25; 22:13; 24:30-34; 26:13-16; 31:27), so we have an opportunity to get a full description of this person's character.

We begin with the verses in our text (24:30-34). These verses are in the form of a story that is very similar to the instructional material in Proverbs 1:8–9:18. In the earlier passage, the instructions are teachable insights that have been gathered by the sages over a long period; the verses in our passage are the result of one particular incident. The author describes an experience he had while out walking, from which he drew a lesson.

On this particular trip, the author passed by a field that belonged to a family known for laziness. He noticed that the field was in a terrible condition. Instead of a beautiful crop that could provide food for the family or produce to sell, he saw weeds and thorns everywhere. The stone wall that farmers typically built to protect their fields from wild animals was broken down in places. The wall was of no use whatsoever. The field had reverted to its original, natural condition before an earlier farmer had cleared and planted it.

The author did not specify what crops were planted in the field. In Proverbs 24:30*a*, he used the word "field," but the parallel in verse 30*b* mentions a "vineyard." Therefore, there could have been either grain or grapevines (or both).

The word "vineyard" immediately brings to mind the parable of the vineyard in Isaiah 5:1-7. As in Proverbs 24:30-34, the vineyard in Isaiah had clearly been neglected. Although God's displeasure in Isaiah was directed at the nations of Israel and Judah, Proverbs focused on a single lazy farmer. In Isaiah, God was disturbed because of a lack of justice and righteousness (5:7), whereas Proverbs 24:30 criticizes a lazy lifestyle.

The lesson the author wanted to teach his readers was that worthwhile accomplishments in life require hard work, diligence, and self-discipline. This is not a new thought. It had been repeated numerous times over the centuries. As early as 1800–1600 BC, Mesopotamians were familiar with this proverb: "As long as a man does not exert himself, he will gain nothing" (*ANET*, 425). By 1550–1300 BC, Egyptians had a similar proverb in *The Instruction of Any*: "He who is slack amounts to nothing" (*AEL*, vol. 2, 139). Today, this proverb is known in the abbreviated form "No pain, no gain."

However, lazy persons never learned these proverbs. They have "an ingrained resistance to working" (Hartley 2016, 90). Thus the life of a lazy person resembles the run-down field of the farmer in Proverbs 24:30-34. Their poor work habits will inevitably lead to troubles in life, such as poverty and hunger. So why would anyone choose to be lazy? The author's answer was that they have "no sense" (v. 30) (lit., "[They are] lacking of heart"). They lack the ability to think rationally and plan for the future. According to verse 33, sleep is more important to them than living a good and useful life. The sages would say that they lack wisdom. Scattered throughout Proverbs are other verses that enlarge on the characteristics of sluggards.

1. Sluggards "Will Not Begin Things" (Kidner 1964, 42)

For most of us, a new day brings new projects and challenges that require lots of energy, hard labor, and sound thinking skills. Sluggards never experience these challenges, because they do not get out of bed in the morning. Like a door that swings on its hinges, the only movement of sluggards is from one side of the bed to the other (Prov. 26:14). Sluggards have no plans to do anything during the day, so why get up? Procrastination is another name for this practice.

2. Sluggards "Will Not Finish Things" (Kidner 1964, 42)

Even when sluggards finally get out of bed and start a project, their enthusiasm quickly dissipates. Proverbs provides three illustrations of this. First, they may go out hunting and catch an animal or a bird, but they are too lazy to cook it (12:27). Second, they may crave something, but they are too lazy to get up and get it (13:4; 21:25-26). Third, while eating, they may reach for some food, but they cannot even bring their hand back to put it in their mouth (19:24; 26:15).

3. Sluggards "Will Not Face Things" (Kidner 1964, 42)

Sluggards live in a fantasy world of their own creation, protected by all kinds of flimsy excuses. One example of such an excuse is that a lion just might be outside their door; it could kill them if they were to venture out (22:13; 26:13). A similar person today might say, "I don't want to go to work today because there will be at least one traffic fatality today and I don't want it to be me" (Murphey 2001, 115).

No one can talk them out of these absurd claims, because they think they are wiser than anyone else (26:16). Sluggards disregard the need to plow and plant their fields at the appropriate time. This refusal to face reality results in dire consequences at harvesttime (10:5; 20:4).

Most of us run into obstacles somewhere along the way of life, but we attempt to clear them away. Sluggards, on the other hand, are too lazy to unclog their pathway. Many of the thorns that block their progress are self-created (15:19). Sluggards refuse to admit it, claiming they are unable to do anything about it.

4. Sluggards Are Worthless to Themselves and Others

Sluggards contribute nothing to their families and communities. Proverbs 10:26 describes them as like "vinegar to the teeth and smoke to the eyes" of their employers. They get in the way of those who really want to work, impeding their progress. At a minimum, they irritate others. But most of the time, they are an obstacle to getting something accomplished.

So what can be done to help sluggards? Maybe nothing. But we must try. One approach is to warn them of the dire consequences of their inaction. This is what Proverbs 24:30-34 tried to do. The run-down field of the sluggard in this passage was a good illustration of the consequences of laziness. These consequences appear suddenly and unexpectedly like a shifty vagabond. They overwhelm sluggards like an armed warrior (v. 34).

Other passages note additional consequences. Lazy people may fall into slavery because of extreme poverty (10:4; 12:24). They may find themselves on the edge of starvation because of a lack of food (19:15). Socially, lazy persons are a disgrace to their families (10:5). The implication is that their families may reject them and render them homeless. They may even die an early death (21:25). Proverbs makes it clear that the consequences of a lazy lifestyle are all negative.

Proverbs 18:9 speaks to another issue—sluggards are no better than those who destroy things. God looks on sluggards as he does on plunderers and thieves. Each receives an appropriate retribution. Implied in this proverb is the principle that sins of omission are just as serious as sins of commission. God expects us to work and to do so diligently. When we do so, he provides for our success. When we refuse, we bring harm to God's kingdom and disaster on ourselves and on our families.

It would be easy for preachers and teachers, after listing the negative consequences in the previous two paragraphs, to leave the mistaken impression that laziness and poverty are always intertwined. It could imply that poor people are poor because they are lazy. But such is not so. Poverty may be one of the results of lazy work habits, but it may be caused by numerous other factors, such as extended illness; natural disasters; recessions; injustice; cultural, social, or political limitations; and so on. Likewise, good work habits do not guarantee riches. Many diligent, hardworking individuals have entered vocations that pay only minimum to modest wages. Through no fault of their own, they may experience low income their entire lives.

A second approach to helping sluggards become industrious is to give them a positive example. Proverbs 6:6-8 takes this approach, pointing to an example everyone knows from nature—the ant. Ants seem to have no boss to order them around, tell them what to do, or when to do it. They just instinctively know what their responsibilities are and do them. The mention of "summer" and "harvest" in verse 8 suggests that humans need to follow the regularity of the seasons, just as the ants do. Winter is the time for plowing and planting in the Near East, and summer is the time for harvesting and storing (see Eccles. 3:1-8). To be successful, humans need to know the seasons God has established and do the work required by that season in life. Ants seem to have that all figured out. Human beings, who appear to be far superior to ants in size and intellect, should order their lives as well.

The problem of laziness is still relevant today. Many people waste hours of time on their phones or in front of their computer screens aimlessly surfing the internet and social media. It can be addictive.

One application of this sermon would be to offer some examples of real persons who have destroyed their lives through laziness. Perhaps someone you knew in high school or college was far too similar to the lazy farmer in Proverbs 24:30-34. One of my college friends ranked as a genius on IQ tests but flunked out after his first year because he never developed the discipline to go to class or read the textbook before exams. Another example was a student in one of my classes whose wife left him after she learned he was spending countless hours and hundreds of dollars on internet pornography.

Another way to apply this sermon would be to present some positive helps for people in your congregation who are struggling with initiative, drive, and stamina. What are some practices you have incorporated into your own life to guard against laziness? I learned that I tended to get sidetracked and slothful when I did not have a to-do list. I needed a reminder in front of me of the activities to be cared for each week. Without a prioritized, written guide listing what needed to be accomplished, I might waste hours just reading interesting but nonessential articles on the internet.

Most of us are not truly lazy. We are just ordinary people trying to earn a living and raise a family. However, we can be tempted to be lazy from time to time, and we all have yielded to it on more than one occasion. We can come up with some pretty good excuses to avoid activities we regard as drudgery—whether homework, housework, or yard work: "I'm tired. I've worked all day. I need a break." Similar excuses can lead us to neglect regular church attendance, devotions, and tithing.

Proverbs repeatedly claims that laziness leads to failure and a meaningless life—one that displeases God. We all need to be on guard against laziness lest we rob ourselves of meaningful success and usefulness to God.

As a final note, all the proverbs dealing with sluggards focus on how laziness affects one's quality of life. Sluggards illustrate the principle that diligent work and adequate preparation are needed to enjoy a successful life. Without preparing their fields in the right season, lazy farmers will have no harvest.

Further, there is a parallel thought in the spiritual realm that preachers and teachers may wish to expand upon in the conclusion. Spiritual laziness in this life will be costly in the next. In fact, without adequate spiritual preparation now, there will be no eternal, joyous life in the life to come. One's spiritual future is dependent on one's present preparation.

Possible Sermon Titles: "No Pain, No Gain," "Lazy Farmers Have No Crops to Sell," "How Much Time Did You Waste This Past Week?" "The Consequences of Avoiding Responsibility," "Lazybones Are Displeasing to God," "There's a Price to Pay for Successful Living," "A Little Sleep, a Little Slumber," "Excuses, Excuses, Excuses," "Look to the Ant!"

VI. MORE SAYINGS ATTRIBUTED TO SOLOMON, WHICH HEZEKIAH PRESERVED (PROV. 25:1–29:27)

A large number of Solomonic proverbs (375) were discussed in chapter 3 (Prov. 10:1–22:16). In Proverbs 25–29 are 138 more verses, also attributed to Solomon. This sixth division of Proverbs has an editorial heading, suggesting why these verses were separated from the earlier ones. As mentioned in the introduction (→ "Introductory Sermon," p. 19), the book of Proverbs is a compilation of smaller collections of sayings. Over time, the main collection grew as additional collections were discovered and added.

Proverbs 25:1 indicates that the sixth division was added in the time of King Hezekiah (two hundred years after Solomon). Most likely, scribes and sages in Hezekiah's court found this forgotten collection and recognized its importance because of its relationship to Solomon. Hezekiah himself may have had a hand in seeing that these verses were added to the growing collection of sayings that eventually became the book of Proverbs.

The sixth division is divided into two sections. A large number of analogies using words such as "as"/"like" and "so"/"thus" characterize Proverbs 25–27. Proverbs 28–29 contain several sayings that use antithetic (contrasting or opposing) parallelism. In terms of content, this latter section includes the greatest number of sayings in the book directed to the king and government officials.

The Paradoxes of Life (Prov. 25:15)

The sages of ancient Israel had a strong desire to make sense out of life. We do too. However, sometimes situations occur that are contrary to common sense and logical lines of reasoning. They are difficult, sometimes even impossible, to explain. An example is our text for today:

> Through patience a ruler can be persuaded,
>> and a gentle tongue can break a bone. (Prov. 25:15)

Our first impulse is to ask, "How can something as soft as our tongue break something hard like a bone?" Logical reasoning tells us that the order should be reversed. Only harder objects can break hard things; softer objects cannot. However, the sages had observed that a gentle tongue is quite powerful (→ earlier sermon "The Power of the Tongue," p. 102). As the main part of our body that is used for speaking, the tongue can build up or destroy (11:11), it can attack or bring healing (12:18), it can turn away wrath or stir up anger (15:1), and it can produce life or crush people's spirits (v. 4). Our speech is also accountable to God, receiving his approval or condemnation (12:22) based on its content and method of delivery.

Proverbs 25:15 is what we would call a paradox—*a situation in life that is contrary to common sense and yet is true.* The sages used this paradox to point out the best way to influence a ruler (or anyone with some level of authority over you, such as your boss). Sometimes when we are passionate about a topic that affects us, we are tempted to stick our bony finger in someone's face, turn up the volume, and tell that person what we think about his or her ridiculous idea or policy. The sages knew that that approach would not work. A person is more likely to succeed by using gentle persuasion and logical reasoning than harsh words and anger. In addition, many leaders do not jump to hasty conclusions or back away easily from policies that they have established. Therefore, patience and gentleness are excellent virtues when trying to influence people who possess power.

There are many other paradoxical sayings in the book of Proverbs. In this sermon, we will look at some of them and then draw some conclusions that apply to our own lives today.

Question: How Can a Person Be Generous and Get Richer?

> One person gives freely, yet gains even more;
>> another withholds unduly, but comes to poverty.
> A generous person will prosper;
>> whoever refreshes others will be refreshed. (Prov. 11:24-25)

Common sense suggests that if you want to increase your wealth, you should hold on to your money and possessions. You should never give them away. Yet the sages had noticed something different about God's order in the world. They had observed that generosity increased one's wealth. Generosity was like a boomerang that returned to bless those who gave to others. Likewise, stinginess also returned to drive people into poverty.

"How can this be?" we ask. "Is this some kind of new math?" No, it is not new math. It is the math that operates in the kingdom of God. The sages wanted to reassure their readers that helping our neighbors will not lead to impoverishment. Rather, it will bring God's blessing on our lives. Centuries earlier, Moses had stressed this point in his address to the Israelites on the plains of Moab (Deut. 15:1-11).

Because these verses are short proverbs, they lack some basic information we would like addressed. For example, *what* should one give (money? time? talent?) and *how much? To whom* should one give (the poor? the church? charities? neighbors?) and *how often?* However, despite lacking this information, we should be able to figure out that God is pleased with people who are generous to others. He is displeased with those who are stingy and tightfisted.

Generosity is an attitude that has to be learned. Original sin creates a tendency toward self-centeredness in all people. Further, the paradoxical nature of generosity producing a benefit for the giver leads many to question whether this principle is true. Perhaps the evidence of generosity's value can be found in the testimonies of those who tithe. The loss of one-tenth of one's income would seem to be a hardship, no matter the amount of one's salary. However, tithing seems to have the opposite effect. It refocuses our basic needs and stretches the distance that our money will go. It also creates an attitude of trust in God that he will always take care of our needs when we put him first in the distribution of our salaries.

Question: How Can Something That Is Stolen Seem Sweet and Then Distasteful?

Food gained by fraud tastes sweet,
> but one ends up with a mouthful of gravel. (Prov. 20:17)

Food is a necessity for every human being. Without it, we would starve. We all have seen pictures of malnourished people from various places around the world. It is a tragedy complicated by natural disasters, climate change, economic failures, political power struggles, and war. The United Nations has made some headway in trying to address the problem, but local political leaders who care little about human needs often tie the hands of those who want to offer much-needed relief.

Proverbs 20:17 is focused on food acquired illegitimately. Whether perpetrated by individuals, businesses, or nations, any food gained by stealing, trickery, exploitation, or lying is fraudulent because it involves stealing—taking something from someone else who needs it for survival.

The first part of the proverb notes that food acquired in this way may taste great at first. The thief may even be excited at his or her craftiness in stealing. The sinful young people in 1:10-14 were genuinely pleased at their ability to harm other people and take their valuables. Likewise, Lady Foolishness claimed that her banquet would be extra sweet and delicious, because the food was stolen (9:13-17).

However, the second part of Proverbs 20:17 describes the complete change in the food's taste—from sweet to disgusting. In fact, it soon tastes like "a mouth full of gravel." It tastes terrible and is inedible. Why the sudden change? Because the food provided only a momentary pleasure, not the lasting satisfaction the thief had envisioned beforehand. The thief may realize that civil laws have been broken, that another family may go hungry because of his or her dastardly deed, and that society may come seeking justice with its punishments. Further, the thief may recognize that moral laws have also been broken. Even if no one else knows, God is aware, and the penalty is death (7:24-27; 9:18). This sudden recognition can be "a vivid analogy for guilt" (Hartley 2016, 216). For a graphic illustration, consider the experience of Rodion Raskolnikov in Fyodor Dostoevsky's novel *Crime and Punishment*.

This proverb is focused on the deceptive acquisition of *food* (also 9:13-18; 23:3; Job 20:12-14), but the principle it teaches could apply to any possession capable of being stolen. Other passages expand the list of items that one might be tempted to steal to include valuables (Prov. 1:10-19), love and sexual gratification (7:6-27), and wine (23:31-32).

The paradox points out a sudden reversal in life always comes to those who choose a life of sin. Sin disguises its consequences from those it is trying to entice. Sinners may be joyful at first that their self-centered activities succeeded. But sooner or later, sinners recognize that they were deceived. Therefore, beware of sin's false enticements. Death, both spiritual and physical, is the final destination of that pathway in life (7:24-27; 9:18).

Question: How Can One Wise Man Be Stronger than a City of Mighty Warriors?

> One who is wise can go up against the city of the mighty
>> and pull down the stronghold in which they trust. (Prov. 21:22)

Proverbs 21:22 illustrates the paradox that wisdom is more powerful than might. This saying celebrates the victory of a single wise man over a strongly fortified city of mighty warriors. Somehow, this man was able to scale a city wall and bring it down so that his fellow soldiers could enter the city and capture it. We are not informed whether the wise man developed a new type of weaponry, discovered a secret entrance to the city, or was able to bribe some citizens into betraying their city. Whatever method he used was effective in capturing the city. His wisdom outwitted a force much greater than himself.

The purpose of this proverb is to show the practical use of wisdom in a time of crisis such as war. The saying is a paradox because the task seems impossible. How can one man conquer a city? He cannot, unless he relies on the wisdom that comes from God.

Ecclesiastes presents a similar story; only in this case, the wise man was inside a city being attacked by outside forces (Eccles. 9:13-18). This one man was able to save his small city from capture because his wisdom was better than deadly "weapons of war" (v. 18).

There are several other examples of this principle in the OT. Joseph used wisdom to feed thousands of Egyptians (and people in neighboring nations) during a severe famine (Gen. 41:1-57). The wise woman of Abel Beth Maakah was able to save her city from destruction by speaking wisely to Joab (2 Sam. 20:14-22). Jonathan and his armor-bearer were able to kill a Philistine outpost of twenty soldiers (1 Sam. 13:23–14:14). David discovered a secret way into Jerusalem, perhaps using a water shaft, and was thus able to capture it (2 Sam. 5:6-8). Esther used her wisdom and courage to save her people from the evil plot of Haman (Esther 3:1–9:19).

Not all of these cases mention wisdom as the factor that brought success, but it is understood that they used godly wisdom and guidance to overcome an impossible situation. Proverbs 21:22 may illustrate how Christ and the church defeat Satan and the forces of evil: "In spite of insurmountable odds, including famine, nakedness, sword (Rom. 8:35) and spiritual forces of evil in heavenly places (Eph. 6:12), Christ built his Church through saints who wear God's armor (Isa. 59:17; Eph. 6:10-18)" (Waltke 2005, 185).

The four paradoxes discussed above illustrate the range of topics found in Proverbs. Here are some additional examples, if preachers and teachers need more:

Question: How Can Beating Children Make Them Better?

> Do not withhold discipline from a child;
>> if you punish them with the rod, they will not die.
> Punish them with the rod
>> and save them from death. (Prov. 23:13-14)

This paradox concerns the importance of parental discipline in raising children.

Question: How Can One Person Reject Honey and Another Long for Something Bitter?

> One who is full loathes honey from the comb,
>> but to the hungry even what is bitter tastes sweet. (Prov. 27:7)

It all depends on timing. How long has it been since your last meal? There is a practical lesson that we can learn from this paradox. It will save us a lot of money. Do not go to the grocery store when you are hungry, or you will probably buy more than you need. Go right after a meal.

Question: How Does Pride in Oneself Humiliate a Person?

> Pride brings a person low,
>> but the lowly in spirit gain honor. (Prov. 29:23)

Here the sage is speaking of the false pride of an overinflated ego. This thought is repeated in 16:18.

There are several examples of paradoxes in the numerical proverbs in Proverbs 30:

- Why are some things never satisfied or brought to completion (vv. 15b-16) (→ the later sermon "Never Enough!" p. 155)?
- Why is it impossible to understand human courtship (vv. 18-19)?
- Why are some people unbearable (vv. 21-23)?
- How can some small animals and insects not only survive but be extremely wise and efficient (vv. 24-28)?
- Why do kings appear to be stately (vv. 29-31)?

Sages sometimes used paradoxes to help readers understand confusing aspects of life. So what are we to learn? Here are two important lessons to keep in mind:

1. Many Situations in Life Are Not What They Seem to Be on the Surface

A job offer may seem attractive because the salary is better, but the working conditions may be more stressful and one's future colleagues may be difficult to work with. A house for sale may appear to be ideal, but a home inspection may reveal that expensive repairs are needed. Advertisements may try to sell us a car or a time-share, but there may be hidden expenses that do not show up until later. Politicians may promise lower taxes, but it most likely comes at the cost of inattention to infrastructure—more potholes and collapsed bridges, fewer services, and cutbacks in educational funding. A modern proverb that echoes these situations is this: "You get what you pay for."

At first glance, some situations seem reasonable and attractive. But life is more complex than simple answers. The sages wanted to look beneath the surface to warn us to be cautious when making major life-changing decisions. They wanted everyone to be aware that some situations in life will always be puzzling. These do not and may never have simple yes or no answers. Does this mean that life is chaotic, unpredictable, and morally relative? No, it means that within God's established order of life on earth, one must make room for paradoxes, exceptions to the rules, and even contradictions. They, too, are a part of our God-ordered existence.

Some situations in life are more than complex and puzzling; they are downright dangerous. The dangers they present are not always evident on the surface. The lurking danger may be concealed due to our tendency to believe that our own opinions are always right (Prov. 14:12; 16:25). We may even try to justify our mistaken opinions, not realizing their basis in ignorance or ungodly motives.

The sages believed that God knows if our pathway is headed toward danger or if our motives and thinking processes are flawed (15:11; 16:2; 21:2). God has a total comprehensive view of our actions, thoughts, and motives. As Fox notes, "God sees even unconscious intentions" (2009, 679). Therefore, our daily prayer should be that of the psalmist in Psalms 139:23-24 or 19:12-14 (13-15 HB).

Several years ago, I spoke in a college chapel about the creation of the earth as revealed in Genesis 1–3. I spoke about the main theological lessons that God wanted us to learn. I noted that all Christians believe that God did it, but there are differences of opinion about how and when it happened. Scientists are still investigating those topics today, and they may always remain puzzling to us.

After chapel, a student came to my office. He was upset with me that I did not have all the answers to creation. He thought that a Christian professor should have an authoritative explanation of how and when creation took place. I could tell that he wanted my answer to be the same as his. He was a person who could not live with a lack of evidence, ambiguity, exceptions, or paradoxes. He was only satisfied with simple yes-and-no answers. He was stuck in a mindset that demanded one clear answer to every issue in life.

Our culture tries to indoctrinate us in various views of life based on politics, business, science, education, religion, or whatever. However, these are only surface perceptions based on incomplete and sometimes erroneous evidence. If we really want to know what reality is like, we must seek God's view of it and reject the world's noise.

The sages had it right when they insisted that "the fear of the Lord [was] the beginning of knowledge" (Prov. 1:7; see Job 28:28). Like it or not, God's ordered world is full of paradoxes, and the sages have helped us recognize and appreciate that.

2. The Greatest Paradox in the Entire Bible Is, Why Should a Holy God Love Imperfect and Sinful People like You and Me?

Holiness and sinfulness are at opposite extremes on the spiritual scale. Therefore, it seems contrary to common sense that a holy God would want anything to do with sinful human beings. But he does. He is continually searching out people, offering to save them from their sins, and then radically changing the present status of their spiritual condition when they confess their sins and accept Christ as their Savior. "How can that be," we ask, "when we have treated God so horribly and acted like his enemy?"

The Bible is full of examples of God's love for sinful people. It started with his allowing Adam and Eve to continue living despite their disobedience. This was followed by God placing a mark on the murdering brother Cain to protect him from being killed in revenge. There is further evidence of his love in his dealings with the Israelites during their exodus from Egypt and wandering through the wilderness. This love continued for centuries during the period of the monarchy and the return from exile in Babylonia.

However, the greatest example of God's love for sinful people is the story of his Son's death on the cross in the Gospels. This is summarized in the most well-known verse in the Bible: "For God so loved the world that he gave his one and only Son, that whoever believes in him shall not perish but have eternal life" (John 3:16). Jesus died for all people, even you and me some two thousand years later. Why did he do so?

This paradox will never have a logically persuasive answer, because it is hidden in the mysteries of God. We know that Jesus's death truly happened. Moreover, we know that its benefits are available to all people who confess their sins (Prov. 28:13-14). Millions have accepted this paradox and found it valid for their lives.

Therefore, the word of wisdom that comes from the NT is this: accept God's love that he freely and lavishly bestowed on you (Eph. 1:8; 1 John 3:1). You may not understand why he loves you—a sinner—for it is a paradox. However, your salvation is dependent on believing that this paradox is true for you.

Possible Sermon Titles: "Surface Perceptions Are Often Wrong," "Let's Dig Deeper," "God's Love Is a Paradox," "Making Sense out of Life," "Making Sense out of Confusing Situations"

VII. SAYINGS ATTRIBUTED TO AGUR (PROV. 30:1-33)

The last two chapters of Proverbs (30–31) are generally considered to be three appendixes. Whether they were added by the final editor(s) of the book or added in various stages is unknown. Apparently, whoever added these small collections of sayings considered them of sufficient value to be included among Israel's wisdom literature.

Proverbs 30 contains an editorial heading (v. 1), which attributes the entire chapter to a man named "Agur son of Jakeh." This is the only place in the Bible where these two names are mentioned, so we know nothing else about them.

The Hebrew word that follows the name of the author (*hammaśśā'*) has been translated in two ways. The NJPS treats it as a proper name—"[man of] Massa." Other versions regard it as the word for "oracle" (e.g., NRSV; "an inspired utterance" [NIV]). Commentators are divided on the correct translation. I lean toward the NJPS translation. If the word is a proper name, it could refer to one of Ishmael's sons (Gen. 25:14; 1 Chron. 1:30). In that case, Agur was a non-Israelite living in northern Arabia who worshipped Israel's God Yahweh (Prov. 30:9). He was also probably elderly and thought he had little time left to live (v. 7). The term "Massa" appears again in 31:1 (NJPS).

Scholars also debate whether Agur's words should be limited to Proverbs 30:1-4, verses 1-9, verses 1-14, or the entire chapter (see the commentaries for a discussion of the issue). If the last position is correct (and I think it is), then Agur is the author of 30:15-16, which is the basis for the sermon below. Otherwise, the author is unknown. There is no evidence concerning the date when Agur lived.

In the first half of Proverbs 30, Agur confesses his lack of wisdom. He then prays to God asking to be kept free of lying and requesting God's help in meeting his basic needs. The second half of the chapter contains a series of numerical proverbs.

Never Enough! (Prov. 30:15–16)

The leech has two daughters.
> "Give! Give!" they cry.

There are three things that are never satisfied,
> four that never say, "Enough!":

the grave, the barren womb,
> land, which is never satisfied with water,
> and fire, which never says, "Enough!" (Prov. 30:15-16)

There are two separate proverbs in this passage, but the verse numbering divides them incorrectly. Verse 15*a* is the first proverb; verses 15*b*-16, the second. They were probably placed side by side because both speak of things that are never satisfied.

I chose these proverbs because they are different from others we have studied. First, a non-Israelite author named Agur wrote them. Second, they give us the opportunity to investigate proverbs that use numerical patterns.

Numerical proverbs usually contain two numbers. One number is given followed by the next highest number. In this case, the numbers three and four are used. There are other examples in the OT of one/two, two/three, four/five, five/six, six/seven, and seven/eight (see Bowes 2018, 122).

Hebrew poets used these patterns to organize a series of items that had some type of relationship with one another. The higher number was the more important. The smaller number was mentioned for rhetorical effect. Sometimes the sage used the last item in the list as a punch line (e.g., Prov. 30:18-19 and vv. 29-31). Number patterns were popular in ANE wisdom literature, but they also appear in some of the prophets (e.g., Amos 1:3–2:8). Perhaps, number patterns were "used both to create interest and to aid with memory" (Gowan 1980, 103). They may have functioned like more recent three-point sermon outlines. But they also may have been used simply for rhetorical effect.

The first proverb in our passage (Prov. 30:15a) uses the image of a leech to describe the greediness of some people. Leeches are a type of worm with a sucker at each end. They attach themselves to a living organism and suck blood from their host. When full of blood, they fall off. Doctors have used certain kinds of leeches for twenty-five hundred years to extract blood from human patients. The "two daughters" are probably a metaphor for the leech's two suckers. A "leech" is applied metaphorically in this passage to people who have a parasitic nature. They "attach themselves to others in order to drain them of their resources" (Longman 2006, 528) and then demand even more.

"They cry" is not in the Hebrew, but it is added in some translations to make clear that the word "Give" is what they are saying. Scholars are divided as to whether "Give" is what the daughters say (NIV, NRSV) or their actual names (GNT, NJPS). Nevertheless, both interpretations result in the same meaning, for the word aptly sums up their character. They constantly sponge off others to acquire successfully what they want, instead of working hard themselves.

The second proverb in the passage (30:15b-16) contains four examples of appetites that are never satisfied with what they have. The first is Sheol, the Hebrew name for the place of the dead (see comments on Sheol in Bowes 2024, 113, and Bowes 2018, 86-87). Everyone will die eventually. In this example, Sheol is personified as one with a ravenous appetite; it constantly gobbles up human beings by the thousands. It will never say "Enough" until all humanity is in the grave. Proverbs 27:20 reinforces this thought.

The second example, "the barren womb" (lit., "closure of the womb"), refers to childless, married women. Their emotional pain and shame will continue as long as they are without children. They will never stop asking God for children, because in ancient times their worth as wives was mainly dependent on their ability to bear children. The Bible contains several examples of women in this situation: Rachel (Gen. 30:1, 22-23), Hannah (1 Sam. 1:9-20), and Elizabeth (Luke 1:24-25). This was also the predicament of Lemuel's mother in Proverbs 31:2.

The third item in the list is dry soil that never ceases to soak up water. Of course, this is not entirely true, for soil can become saturated and begin to feed streams, which flow into rivers, which empty into the ocean. A flood can even completely saturate soil. Still, the imagery is valid in normal conditions.

The fourth example of something that is never satisfied is fire. A fire will continue to burn until all combustible material is turned into ashes.

The theme of the two proverbs is the selfish, insatiable greed of some people to add more to what they already have. They never have enough. There is a feeling of incompleteness that drives them to seek more fulfillment. It is this sense of incompleteness that sometimes causes people to sponge off others in order to fulfill their desires.

God created human beings to live ordered, disciplined lives that follow his guidance. If we do so, we will find great satisfaction in the progress and success of our lives. However, those who choose to live selfish lives, obsessed with personal gain and the unending accumulation of things, will never be content.

At first glance, these two proverbs seem entirely secular. This is just a commonsense understanding of life. To live a good life, people should discipline their urges. However, the sages viewed commonsense guidelines as instructions from God about how to live. If God created the world and ordered everything in it, then his commonsense guidelines need to be followed.

Unfortunately, these two proverbs make no direct application to humanity. They state their condemnation of greed only in broad principles and through metaphors. The author's intent was to challenge us to think about it and make the application to our own lives. In doing so, we may discover a need to make some changes in our actions and/ or attitudes. If our knowledge about this topic is increased, then we will be more equipped to make good choices in the future when presented with similar options.

The author probably wants us to ask ourselves questions such as these: Are there aspects of my life that seem unfulfilled? In pursuit of fulfillment, am I engaging in activities that are unwholesome or destructive to others or myself? If so, I am acting in unwise ways. I am no better than the fire that devours everything in its path to be satisfied. Instead of acting in purposeful ways that are guided by God, I am driven by insatiable urges that seek selfish gains. No doubt, the author was thinking here of the human pursuit of things such as wealth, power, recognition, and love. Aptly, the advertising industry refers to potential customers as consumers.

The quest to acquire more things can become all-consuming and unending. Many people fall prey to such obsessions. No matter how much wealth they have, they always desire more. Toward the end of his life in the early twentieth century, John D. Rockefeller was the richest man on earth. When asked how much money was enough, he reportedly answered, "Just a little bit more." First Timothy 6:6-10 speaks to this same issue, encouraging people to live lives of contentment rather than greed.

In developing the sermon, one way to overcome the lack of an application is to draw upon other verses in the wisdom literature and the Bible as a whole that speak to the topic of greed in general. Here are some additional passages that could be fashioned into several points of the sermon:

- Greed originates in a wicked heart (Prov. 21:26; Mark 7:21-22; Rom. 1:28-32).
- Greed destroys a person's life (Prov. 1:19; Luke 12:13-21).
- Greed causes trouble, especially in one's household (Prov. 15:27; 28:25; James 4:1-3).
- Greed for pleasure and money provides no satisfaction (Eccles. 2:10-11; 5:10-12; 1 Tim. 6:10; Heb. 13:5).

Another way to deal with the lack of an application is to expand the topic. "Covetousness," "envy," and "lust" are partial synonyms of "greed." These words have slightly different meanings that need to be defined, but they all broadly refer to a desiring, craving, or yearning for something that belongs to another. Greed differs from them in that it seeks the accumulation of items *beyond* what a person really needs. Coveting, on the other hand, may occur for something a person really needs.

A third way to preach and teach these two proverbs is to connect them with the tenth commandment (Exod. 20:17; Deut. 5:21). The tenth commandment itemizes several different possessions that could become the objects of one's coveting. They include a neighbor's house, spouse, slaves, and animals. Then it goes on to state that anything that belongs to your neighbor can become an object of coveting. In today's world, we might mention things such as power, popularity, position, personality, possessions, appearance, honors, and achievements as possible objects of coveting.

Greed and coveting may be "secret sins." They refer to an inward attitude of the heart. No one will ever know you have coveted, except God. However, there is only a short distance between the desire and actions that are taken to fulfill that desire. In other words, if you develop a craving for something (such as chocolate), you are probably going to think about it a lot and scheme about how you are going to get it. The result may involve sinful, outward activities.

We have all seen this principle in operation among children. Put two children in the same room, each with a different collection of toys. What happens? Each child wants the other child's toys. However, it does not just stop with a desire. Each child is going to do something to get the other child's toys. He or she is going to walk or crawl over to the other child and start playing with that child's toys without asking to do so.

As children grow older, their parents teach them some principles about sharing. By the time they are into their teens, they should have learned to refrain from stealing their friends' toys. Yet the heart attitude of coveting may not have disappeared. It may only be covered up, hidden within. There is still a lot of envy and coveting that goes on in high school over appearance, clothing, cars, grades, and especially boyfriends and girlfriends. How many disagreements or fights break out in high school, or how much gossiping takes place whose root cause is coveting? Unfortunately, coveting is a practice that many adults continue, sometimes with deadly consequences. For some biblical examples of the consequences of greed and coveting, see the following: Adam and Eve (Gen. 3:1-7), Shechem (34:1-3), Potiphar's wife (39:6-12), Achan (Josh. 7:1, 20-21), David (2 Sam. 11:1-5), Amnon (13:1-14), and Ahab and Jezebel (1 Kings 21:1-14).

How you develop your sermon will determine the way you prepare to conclude the message.

Possible Sermon Titles: "God's View of Greed," "A Numerical Proverb on Greed," "Human Leeches," "Leeches in Human Form," "Obsessed with More"

VIII. SAYINGS ATTRIBUTED TO KING LEMUEL (PROV. 31:1-9)

The author of this collection of Proverbs is called "Lemuel, king of Massa" (Prov. 31:1, NJPS). Massa was also the home of Agur in the preceding section (30:1-33), but it is unknown if there was any relationship between the two. All we know about Lemuel is that he was a non-Israelite, living in northern Arabia. What is unique about Lemuel's sayings is that he learned them from his mother. No other sayings in Proverbs are identified as feminine in origin, although it is possible that others are.

In Proverbs 31:2, Lemuel's mother expresses her thankfulness that God gave her a son. Her words indicate that Lemuel was probably another OT example of a late-born son who was conceived in answer to his mother's fervent prayers. If so, her prayers may have been similar to Hannah's, who prayed for a son in the presence of Eli the priest (1 Sam. 1:9-11). In Proverbs 31:3-9, Lemuel's mother gave her son three brief words of advice: (1) avoid carousing with women, (2) avoid alcoholic beverages, and (3) look out for the needy. Apparently, she recognized that success in life could cause one to forget principles that were taught earlier in the home.

The main reason I have chosen to craft a sermon out of this brief passage is because it speaks well to one of the main themes in Proverbs—order. Lemuel's mother put her finger on this topic in a very forceful way. She knew that even if she raised her son well, the trappings of royal power could break down his integrity and lead him into a self-centered, disordered life of sin and corruption. Therefore, this sermon focuses on the profound sense of order God has embedded in his creation. We draw on a number of verses from elsewhere in Proverbs to enlighten further the words of advice from Lemuel's mother.

Order in the Court (Prov. 31:1-9)

We have all seen enough courtroom scenes unfold on television to know that order is an essential part of judicial proceedings.

(1) There is the order of place. Specific places are assigned for the judge, the jury, the prosecution, the defendant, and visitors to sit.

(2) There is the order of procedure. Judges are the last to enter the courtroom, and everyone in the court must rise when they enter. All witnesses must raise their hands and swear to tell the truth. The prosecuting attorney presents the charges and evidence first, and the defense counsel follows with counterarguments and more evidence.

(3) There is the order of speech. The attorneys on either side are bound by the order of presentation and the rules of legal terminology. Their arguments are carefully crafted along logical lines of reasoning to lead to a guilty verdict or an acquittal.

(4) There is even the order of dress. The judge wears a judicial robe, and the attorneys wear suits. The plaintiff and the defendant are also usually nicely dressed. Order governs everything that takes place in a courtroom.

Lemuel's mother was also aware of the need for order in a person's life—specifically her son's. If our reading of this passage is correct, Lemuel's father was probably a king and Lemuel inherited that position from his father.

Consequently, Lemuel's mother had known for a long time that her son would one day be king of Massa. No doubt, she had planned for this event for years, and she had taken the time to instruct him in good principles of leadership and personal integrity. Once he became king, she reminded him of some of her teachings through this short passage in Proverbs 31:1-9.

The many writers who contributed to the book of Proverbs were also concerned about order in everyday life. They mentioned it hundreds of times in their short sayings that eventually became incorporated into Proverbs. They believed that God had embedded his order into every facet of life on earth. People could discover this order simply by observing the objects and activities around them. As a result, they invested much effort in examining the natural world, the world of human behavior, the world of social interaction, and the world of morality, looking for principles and patterns that God had woven into the universe. In effect, they were some of the world's first scientists—looking at life and creating explanations that helped people understand the world in which they lived and how to be successful in it. In this sermon, we look at some of the many facets of order the sages discovered in our world.

1. The Natural World

God ordered the natural world at the time of creation, and this order has continued ever since. Genesis 1–2 is the usual OT passage that we turn to for support of this concept. Proverbs also has two important passages (3:19-20; 8:22-31) that enlarge upon the Genesis presentation. Both stress that God used his wisdom (and understanding and knowledge) to fashion the natural world.

Our universe was not haphazardly put together. God had a blueprint to guide him in how the world should look and operate. The order we see today in the watery depths and the seas, in the mountains and farmers' fields, and in the clouds and heavens was there from the time God created them (Prov. 8:24-29). Proverbs 8 adds the unique personification of wisdom as a lady who was created first and then used by God to create the rest of the world.

The other wisdom books in the OT also support this concept of God's order in the natural world. In Job, God himself speaks of the actions he took to bring the world into existence (38:4-11). He "laid the earth's foundation" (v. 4), he "marked off its dimensions" (v. 5), he "laid its cornerstone" (v. 6), he "shut up the sea behind doors" (v. 8), and so on.

Then God describes how he continues to operate the world according to ordered principles (vv. 12-38). He controls day and night, the seasons, the deepest depths of the sea as well as the stars in the heavens, and the weather.

Finally, God extends his order to the animal kingdom. The author describes various characteristics that he gave to eleven animals and birds—the lion, the raven, the mountain goat, the wild ass, the wild ox, the ostrich, the horse, the hawk, the eagle, the hippopotamus, and the crocodile (38:39–39:30; 40:15–41:34).

Proverbs comments on God's order in the animal kingdom using ants, eagles, snakes, rock badgers, locusts, and lizards as examples (6:6-8; 30:18-19, 24-31). God knows all about these creatures, because he ordered their lives when he brought them into being. Furthermore, he likes them just the way they are.

In the book of Ecclesiastes, God's order is extended to time. There are fourteen pairs of opposites in 3:1-8. These include a variety of human activities from birth to death and war to peace. The point is that God controls the progression of time (see the sermon "In His Time" in Bowes 2025, 51).

All of these passages from the wisdom books make clear that there is order in the natural world as a result of God's actions in creation. Because of this orderliness, we know that our world has stability, regularity, and purpose.

2. The World of Human Behavior

The observations of human behavior the sages noted taught them that certain attitudes and practices should be avoided to achieve a good life.

The first is anger. Anger stirs up conflict (Prov. 15:1, 18; 29:22). It can become cruel and overwhelming if not controlled (27:4). People can easily become angry if they hang around those who are "quick-tempered" (14:17, 29). Fiery individuals drag others down with them, and soon they are all angry (22:24-25). Therefore, people should pick their companions carefully. Patience, self-control, and overlooking a wrong are additional ways to avoid anger (16:32; 19:11).

Second, the sages warned against jealousy, envy, and craving. They especially urged the wise not to envy wicked people. They are violent troublemakers without any hope for the future (3:31; 23:17-18; 24:1-2, 19-20). One proverb states, "envy rots the bones" (14:30). In other words, we are headed for an early death if we become entrapped in envy (24:20).

A person might be tempted to envy while visiting the homes of rich people who have lots of possessions. But if these people are stingy, they will offer choice food but not really provide it. In fact, they become upset with visitors for using up some of their wealth (23:6-8).

Third, do not seek revenge. Wait for God to punish those who harm you (20:22; 24:29).

Fourth, avoid anxiety. It "weighs down the heart" (12:25).

The fifth attitude to avoid is a haughty spirit (arrogance/false pride). Fools and mockers tend to be arrogant (18:2; 21:24), but their actions are disgraceful (11:2). They continually cause strife and fall into sin (13:10; 21:4). They are headed for an early downfall (16:18; 18:12). A haughty spirit puffs up one's sense of self-importance, but God prefers the "lowly in spirit" (16:19; 29:23). Arrogance is one of the attitudes God detests most (6:16-17; 16:18-19). He will see to the destruction of those who act this way (15:25; 16:5).

On the positive side, the sages urged people to practice four behavioral characteristics.

The first is a teachable attitude. It is the opposite of a haughty spirit. A teachable attitude begins in the home with instructions from Mom and Dad. This admonition is repeated several times in the first seven chapters of Proverbs, beginning with 1:8:

Listen, my son, to your father's instruction
   and do not forsake your mother's teaching.

Parents have the opportunity to train their children in this most important life skill. If their children incorporate this skill into their lives, they will become wise (9:9; 13:1, 10, 13-14) and knowledgeable (12:1; 18:15). However, if they refuse to listen or take advice, they will cease to be wise and knowledgeable (19:27).

Sometimes a parent's instructions include correction and discipline. This may not be pleasant, but it is necessary for children to learn and mature (13:18; 15:5, 10, 31-32; 17:10; 19:25). Once children have learned how to accept discipline in the home, they will be better prepared to accept it from God (3:11-12). Eliphaz expanded on this idea in Job 5:17-27.

A second positive, behavioral characteristic is humility—putting others before oneself (Prov. 15:33; 18:12).

A third characteristic is joy. A joyful heart produces a cheerful face (15:13), and a cheerful face is good medicine for the discouraged and fearful (17:22). Those who are experiencing troubles in life and need encouragement should spend some time with a joyful person, not a sourpuss. Then they should attempt to be joyful themselves. Two types of people who experience joy are peacemakers (12:20) and the righteous (10:28). The sages encouraged all their readers to be both.

The fourth positive behavioral characteristic is love. According to the sages, love is more important than wealth (15:17). Even the poor can enjoy a good life if they have love for others. Love is also valuable in dealing with hurtful social interactions (10:12; 17:9). People with a loving spirit will not seek revenge against someone who does them wrong. Rather, they will seek the best interests of the one who offended them.

The most valuable part of love is that it provides an atonement for sin (16:6). Since only God can forgive sin, seemingly the word "love" in this verse applies to God. However, the parallel phrase in verse 6b ("the fear of the LORD") is a human activity. Therefore, it seems best to credit "love and faithfulness" in verse 6a to humans as well.

The meaning of the verse, then, is that our love and faithfulness to God and others enables him to atone for any of our sins that result from bad human behavior.

3. The World of Social Interaction

There is also an order that God intended for the interactions between human beings. Here are some of the guidelines the sages proposed for getting along with others.

First, when interacting with other people, we should avoid conflicts and quarreling as much as possible. It is better to be at peace and have little than to have much and live in strife (Prov. 17:1). In fact, it is even an honor to avoid conflict (20:3). Some people are naturally quarrelsome (26:21). They include sinners/the wicked (17:19; 22:5), hotheaded people (15:18), fools (18:6), and haughty people (13:10). Stay away from them at all costs.

The wise are careful to prevent or stay clear of situations that can lead to conflict, such as "hate (10:12), impatience (15:18), gossip (16:28), mocking (22:10), drunkenness (23:29-30), greed (28:25), and anger (29:22)" (Longman 2006, 555). If it is impossible to avoid strife, we should make sure our quarreling is for a good reason (3:30). Hurt feelings are not a good reason. Do not be tempted to get involved in someone else's quarrels; to do so is only asking for trouble (26:17).

Finally, we should note that God detests anyone "who stirs up conflict in the community" (6:19).

Second, we should never engage in lying, deception, or betrayal. This is another human activity detested by God (3:32; 11:20; 12:22). Deceivers are unreliable (25:19) and attracted to violence (13:2). Even if you only intended your words as a joke, the recipient of your deception may interpret your speech as a personal attack (26:18-19). Eventually deceivers will be trapped by their own evil ways (11:6). God will see that they are destroyed (v. 3; 13:15).

There are two situations where lying and deception are especially harmful to others. One is in the world of commerce where goods are being bought and sold, and the other is in the courtroom.

Regarding commerce, there are four proverbs condemning the practice of putting false weights on the scales (11:1; 16:11; 20:10, 23). This was an easy way for merchants to deceive buyers to gain more profit. Another proverb relating to commercial activity condemns greed and the paying of bribes to gain an advantage (15:27). The most frequently condemned commercial activities were the lending of money and the promise to stand good for a neighbor's debt (6:1-2; 11:15; 17:18; 20:16; 22:7, 26-27; 27:13). The latter may seem to be a compassionate, neighborly thing to do to help a friend through a difficult time. But the sages noted that these practices left people vulnerable. The lender and the borrower were now in a business relationship rather than just a friendship. If the borrower came on hard times and could not repay the debt, their friendship would likely suffer. Therefore, the sages recommended for people to be generous and just give friends the money they really need rather than lend it (11:24-26).

The courtroom is another place where absolute honesty is essential to maintaining the divine order. A courtroom exists to determine the truth and to administer justice. It is not the place to get even (24:28-29), to share confidential information (25:9-10), or to cover up the truth (12:17; 14:5). False witnesses are not interested in justice (19:28). Instead of saving lives, false witnesses destroy the innocent (14:25; 18:5). Because God is just and longs for justice on earth, he detests false witnesses (6:19) and promises to punish them (19:5; 21:28).

Third, we should respect the integrity of other people and protect their reputations. Gossiping or whispering behind another person's back would quickly break up a friendship and lead to conflict (16:28; 26:20).

Fourth, we should actively strive to achieve justice for all people. Justice was important to God and Lady Wisdom (8:14-16, 20-21). It should be important to kings, if they are to provide stability for their countries (16:10; 29:4).

Unfortunately, not all rulers and leaders regard it as necessary, and neither do all ordinary people. Wicked people and false witnesses in court care nothing about justice (17:23; 19:28; 21:7; 28:5; 29:9). Injustice is particularly wrong because it harms the poor and innocent (13:23; 18:5). In the end, those who practice injustice will reap calamity (22:8). Only the righteous know what justice is and practice it (12:5; 28:5).

Fifth, we should seek good companions. We all will have companions in life, but not all companions are helpful and supportive. The sages described good companions as righteous (2:20) and wise (13:20). Bad companions are violent (3:31-32), foolish (14:7), gossips (20:19), angry (22:24-25), gluttons and drunkards (23:20-21), wicked (24:1-2), rebellious (vv. 21-22), and flatterers (29:5). People such as this will drag you down to their level and destroy your life. Proverbs 1:10-19 describes how young people can become entangled with bad companions and end up in deep trouble.

Sixth, Proverbs even has advice concerning interactions with our enemies. God will help us to find a way to be at peace with them (16:7), not to rejoice when they fall (24:17-18), and to feed them when they are hungry (25:21-22).

4. The World of Morality

Proverbs makes it very clear that there are moral decisions human beings must make in life. Good and evil pathways do exist in our world, and humans must choose on which road they will travel. People on the good pathway fear and trust in the Lord (3:5-8; 16:20; 19:23), live "blameless lives" (20:7), "pursue righteousness" (15:9), and seek wisdom (8:35-36). God blesses those who choose the right pathway and live this way. This blessing even carries over to the next generation, for their children are blessed too (20:7).

Eight verses in Proverbs pronounce blessings on those who fear God and live godly and wise lives (3:13, 18; 8:32, 34; 16:20; 20:7; 28:14; 29:18). There is an additional blessing for those who are "kind to the needy" (14:21). Verses that offer blessings are called beatitudes. They are worded like Jesus's beatitudes in the Sermon on the Mount (Matt. 5:3-12).

On the negative side, Proverbs lists several human activities God hates. They are an abomination (*tôʿēbâ*) to him. These fourteen passages describe "practices that Yahweh considers to be contrary to his holy character. In committing such an offense a person's behavior is an affront to God" (Hartley 2016, 93).

These offenses include the perverse or corrupt (Prov. 3:32; 11:20), "a heart that devises wicked schemes" and "feet that are quick to rush into evil" (6:18; see vv. 16-19), dishonest scales (11:1; 20:10, 23), "lying lips" (12:22), the "sacrifice of the wicked" (15:8; 21:27), the "way of the wicked" (15:9), the "thoughts of the wicked" (v. 26), the "proud of heart" (16:5), injustice in the court (17:15), and the prayers of the disobedient to God (28:9). The seriousness of these practices is seen when they are compared to practices in the law that use the same wording: "idolatry (Deut 7:25; 27:15), sacrificing blemished animals (Deut 17:1), and sacrificing children (Deut 12:31)" (Hartley 2016, 93).

In conclusion, the principal theme that ties all the hundreds of sayings together in the book of Proverbs is the profound sense of order God embedded throughout his creation. God intended for order to be found in the natural world, the social world, the moral world, and especially within our own characters.

Does order characterize our society today? If we consider the United States as an example, our world is pretty mixed up right now, lacking sanity and clarity. The first twenty years of the twenty-first century for the United States have been extremely stressful. Experiences have included (1) a polarized society and ineffective political leaders; (2) wickedness and corruption in high places; (3) a physical attack against society on September 11, 2001; (4) immigration issues at the southern border; (5) a pandemic that has taken the lives of more than a million Americans; (6) racial injustice and unrest; (7) growing financial inequality among citizens; (8) a large increase in the national debt; (9) climate issues that affect the entire planet; and

(10) a Russian war of aggression in Ukraine and military tensions with China, Iran, and North Korea.

Some places cannot have civil school board meetings without fights and yelling. Many people do not even know what truth is anymore because so much ignorant and biased misinformation circulates on the internet. Even the church has been affected. Some Christians have let themselves get caught up in the passions and anger of political parties and personal preferences, while neglecting to live out the Golden Rule. The point is this: Can we still believe that God's order is even possible in contemporary society?

Before answering that question, we should note that the book of Proverbs says very little about big-picture issues affecting modern society. Some of our issues, such as climate change and pandemics, were not even on the edge of the "radar screens" of the ancient sages.

Even more significantly, sages dealt with societal issues by addressing individual issues first. The sages were mainly interested in promoting individual behavior that was godly and wise. If every Israelite would live a life that was pleasing to God, then the big issues would get resolved. God would watch over Israel and help the Israelites deal with whatever problems came along.

Therefore, the answer to the question about whether God's order is possible in any society is yes. According to the sages, the question has to be addressed at the individual level before society can be changed. If individuals will let God change their prejudices and sinful self-centeredness and will follow God's way for their lives, then God will help them bring order to society as a whole.

The fear of the LORD leads to life;
> then one rests content, untouched by trouble. (Prov. 19:23)

Society in Jesus's day was no less corrupt than today. Just like the sages, Jesus recognized that it could be changed from within if individuals would change spiritually. He encouraged his followers to be salt and light (Matt. 5:13-14) and to be as pervasive as mustard seeds and yeast (13:31-33). Their numbers might be few, and their political clout small and even unseen. But Jesus seemed to believe that their power would be effective, little by little. Even though our world may seem very sinful and hopeless at times, Jesus left us with these words of encouragement: "With God all things are possible" (19:26).

King Lemuel's mother recognized that order needed to be a significant part of her son's life. It would determine whether he was personally successful as a king and whether his country of Massa did well. Her words are preserved in Scripture, not so much for their content—none of us is going to become a king, but because they serve as a reminder that God's order needs to be the blueprint for all our life's activities.

Because God carefully planned this world and ordered its parts in sensible ways, we can trust him to order our own lives as well. Job finally came to this same conclusion after God had taken him on a guided tour of the universe (Job 42:1-6).

So how ordered is your life? Does it measure up to the standards of human behavior that the ancient Israelite sages taught? Is it reflected in your social interactions with other people? Are you on the right moral pathway that God has laid out for you and all other human beings? The sages' word of advice is this:

Trust in the LORD with all your heart
> and lean not on your own understanding;
in all your ways be in a right relationship with him [i.e., know
> him, trust him, love him, worship him],
and he will make and keep your pathway straight and smooth.
> (Prov. 3:5-6, author's paraphrase)

Possible Sermon Titles: "Lemuel's Marching Orders from His Mother," "How Ordered Is Your Life?" "A Mother's Word of Advice," "God's Plans for Order"

IX. THE VIRTUOUS WOMAN (PROV. 31:10-31)

One of the most well-known passages in Proverbs is the poem in the last chapter on the virtuous woman. Most churchgoers have probably heard at least one sermon from this text on Mother's Day. In addition, they may have heard preachers appeal to it as an ideal model for all godly women to follow. No doubt, most women in the congregation left the service feeling totally inadequate. No woman can live up to all the ideals in this passage.

However, the passage was most likely written to young men, not women. It provides a list of feminine qualities that a man should think about in his search for a wife. The sages hoped he would consider these ideals as important, even if he never found one woman who measured up to all of these characteristics.

A Woman to Be Praised (Prov. 31:10–31)

Proverbs 31:10-31 is a self-contained poem that was added to the book as its third and final appendix. It is one of several OT poems that use an acrostic format (see Pss. 9–10, 25, 34, 37, 111, 112, 119, 145; Lam. 1, 2, 3, 4). In an acrostic poem, each line begins with the successive letters of the Hebrew alphabet in their correct alphabetical order. Since the Hebrew alphabet has twenty-two letters, the poem has twenty-two verses. Poets who used the acrostic format had to be some of the most skilled poets in any language. Every language has a few letters that are rarely used (e.g., in English there are few words that begin with x and z). The author of Proverbs 31:10-31 was able to master this format while still sticking closely to his topic and creating a beautiful poem. Davis aptly describes this literary creation as singing "the lady's praises 'from A to Z'" (2000, 151).

There are no stanzas in this poem. An introductory verse introduces the topic (v. 10), and four closing verses emphasize the praise due the ideal woman from her family and community (vv. 28-31). Because the structure is mainly guided by the acrostic format, the result is necessarily a somewhat random order of topics on the woman's character, her deeds, and her value.

Our sermon starter analyzes each individual verse, before drawing some conclusions and applying them to a modern audience.

Proverbs 31:10

The passage begins with a question about a certain kind of woman. Some versions call her "a capable wife" (NRSV). But the verses that follow indicate that she is much more than merely capable; she is a superwoman. The Hebrew is literally "woman of strength" (*hayil*).

The word in other contexts refers to strength in a variety of ways: "in wealth, physical power, military might, practical competencies, or character" (Fox 2009, 891). Military strength applied only to men in ancient times, but all the other attributes apply to this woman. She is a strong, virtuous, and talented woman of tremendous energy. No one word can fully encapsulate her character. We use "virtuous" because she is virtuous in so many ways—in character, in compassion, in vigor, in wisdom, and in morality.

The description of this virtuous woman begins with a question: Who can find such a woman? The question is rhetorical. It could mean that such a woman is impossible to find, or such women are rare. Since this passage was probably written to young men, the question most likely implied rarity. The author did not want his readers to quit looking for such a woman. Rather, the author wanted them to think carefully about the qualities of character they should seek in a future wife. They should not rush into marriage. They should wait until they found the right woman, a woman whose value was priceless.

Proverbs 31:11-12

Trust is a vital ingredient in the recipe for a successful marriage. This marriage had plenty of it. The woman's husband knew his wife would run their household well and even add to their family income through her industriousness. As a result, he was free to participate in a leadership role in the community (v. 23). He was confident that her one goal was to bring good to their family.

Proverbs 31:13

This verse begins a list of activities in which the virtuous woman is engaged. There is no attempt to rank the importance of each item. The first is securing wool and flax for use in making clothing for her household and others (vv. 19, 21-22, 24). She may have secured her supply of wool from her own farm or purchased it from neighbors. Egypt was a major producer of flax, so she may have purchased these supplies from traveling Egyptian merchants. Only the wealthy could afford linen (made from flax) to make their clothing.

Proverbs 31:14-15

Typical of ancient practices, most of the food this woman prepared for her family came from their family-owned land and nearby local farms. She may have purchased a few products from traveling traders. She was diligent in keeping her family and servants well fed. She got up early in the morning to get a good start on the day.

There are two ways to translate the Hebrew *ḥōq* in verse 15c. The NRSV interprets it as the instructions the woman gave her maids. However, the NIV probably chooses the better interpretation as "portions" (of food). This is an early indication that the woman's family is affluent; they have servants.

Proverbs 31:16

The buying and selling of property was normally handled by men in the ancient world. But this remarkable woman was a shrewd real estate entrepreneur. Once she had acquired new property, she quickly had it planted, using money she has earned from her trading and sewing (vv. 18, 24). In verse 16, the verb "considers" (*zmm*) implies careful thought and the formulation of a value judgment about the quality of the field.

Proverbs 31:17-18

These two verses praise the woman's strength and vigor. She was a tireless worker by day and by night. Verse 18b can be interpreted in two ways. One way is to continue the emphasis on her incredible

IX. THE VIRTUOUS WOMAN

capacity for work, using a metaphor. She worked well into the night in addition to rising early (v. 15). The other interpretation points out her diligence in keeping the house illuminated at night. She had to get up at least once every night to fill the lamps with oil. By either interpretation, her sleep suffered.

Proverbs 31:19

Here we see one of the ways the virtuous woman earns money. She spun thread from wool and flax (v. 13), which she then wove into cloth (vv. 22, 24). In verse 19, her tools were the spindle (*kîšôr*; "distaff" [NIV]) and the spindle-whorl (*pelek*; "spindle" [NIV]) (Fox 2009, 895). This woman most likely used servants to do this for her, but apparently, she also did it herself.

Proverbs 31:20

The busy hands that were involved in industry in verse 19 are used for charity in verse 20. She reached out to the needy in her community. What she gave them is not mentioned. We can only surmise from the other verses that she offered them needed food and clothing.

Proverbs 31:21-22

Snow is not a regular occurrence in most of the Near East. When it comes, some people are ill prepared for the complications it creates. The family of the virtuous woman, though, was ready; she had made them appropriate clothing to keep them warm ahead of time.

The word "scarlet" or "crimson" (*šānîm*) refers to a color worn only by the affluent, not to the warmth of a garment. A slight adjustment of the letters (emendation) might allow the word to be translated "double." This would indicate she made clothing with a double layer for extra warmth (Longman 2006, 545; Murphy 1998, 247). This may be correct. But the verse may simply have indicated "that even clothes meant for warmth are luxurious" in appearance (Fox 2009, 896).

Both the warm clothing and regular clothing reveal that this was a wealthy family. Verse 22 confirms this. Only the rich wore purple clothing made from fine linen. The dye had to be imported from the coastal area of Phoenicia.

Proverbs 31:23

This is the only verse in the passage that speaks of her husband's activities. All the others highlight the virtuous woman's skills and talents. The man in this household was prominent in their community. His seat at the city gates was in the company of the other city leaders.

He may have earned this position through several possible means: wealth, good deeds, longevity in the community, and acceptance by the other elders. But his incredible wife was his major asset.

The gate of a city was where important business took place, such as personal contracts, sales of property, marriage arrangements, settlement of disputes, and all community decisions. In the book of Ruth, Boaz met before ten elders at the gate of Bethlehem to arrange the sale of Naomi's property along with his marriage to Ruth (Ruth 4:1-12).

Some have suggested that this man was a no-good husband who spent all his time out in public, leaving his wife to do all the work in the household and farm. Others suggest that his wife was the real power behind the throne. He was only prominent in the city because she ran everything. Recall the modern proverb "Behind every great man is a great woman."

But such views miss the point. The poem was about her, not him. Civic duties were undoubtedly not the only responsibility this man had. He certainly had other tasks at home. His involvement in the community shows that he had a prominent leadership role in the community. Both husband and wife made valuable contributions to their community.

Proverbs 31:24

This verse returns to the woman's business activities. Using the flax she purchased in verse 13, she spins it into thread (v. 19) and then makes linen garments that she sells. By this means, she supplemented the family income. Industrious families in the ancient world often had small cottage industries, as they still do in the two-thirds world today.

In verse 24, the product she made is called a *ḥăgôr*. This was some type of belt or sash worn around the waist. In its only other OT occurrences (1 Sam. 18:4; 2 Sam. 20:8), it refers to a strong belt for hold-

IX. THE VIRTUOUS WOMAN

ing a sword or dagger. Belts made of *linen* were more likely intended for women's clothing. The Hebrew for "merchant" (*kəna'ănî*) originally meant "Canaanite." It probably referred to the Phoenician traders who lived along the Mediterranean coast. They were the sea merchants of the ancient world.

Proverbs 31:25

There are two thoughts in this verse. First, this woman is clothed in "strength and splendor" (NJPS). This is metaphorical language like Job 29:14. Strength and splendor were such a basic part of her character that it seemed she wore them as clothing daily. Second, she was not at all fearful of the future. She did not have to worry about possible calamities that may affect her family; she was well prepared for all contingencies.

Proverbs 31:26

The virtuous woman regarded teaching as one of her responsibilities. The recipients of her teaching were most likely her own children, but she may also have given instructions to her servants. The subject matter of her teaching was "wisdom."

As applied to her children, it probably meant teaching them how to perform basic household tasks, as well as giving them an essential understanding of life from God's perspective. The second clause is literally "the teaching of kindness" (*hesed*). This could refer either to her kindly teaching method or to the teaching content that stressed *hesed* ("love," "loyalty," "faithfulness," "mercy").

Proverbs 31:27

Two thoughts are emphasized here. First, this woman was aware of the needs of her household, and she managed the activities of everyone in her household to meet those needs. Second, there was not a lazy bone in her body. She never stopped until her work was done. "Does not eat the bread of idleness" was a metaphor for avoiding laziness.

Proverbs 31:28-29

The long list of this woman's activities and accomplishments deserved praise. In these two verses, she received this from those who were closest to her. Her children and husband knew exactly what she had contributed to their family; they gladly expressed their deep appreciation and thanks.

Her husband's words in verse 29 voiced what every wife wanted to hear: "There are a lot of good women around, but you are the best wife and mother in the whole wide world" (author's paraphrase). He implied, "I'm sure glad you agreed to marry me, because you are the crown of my life!" (12:4, author's paraphrase).

The interpretation of the first clause in 31:28 is difficult because the meaning of the main verb 'šr is not altogether clear. Translators have struggled with this. The NRSV has the children praising their mother's emotional state: she is "happy." The NIV has them praising her spiritual state: she is "blessed." Other scholars think they are praising her luck: she is fortunate. However, these translations are difficult, because English has no exact equivalent word for the Hebrew verb 'šr.

The children offered their mother "as a model . . . to be envied and imitated" (Waltke 2004, 257, following Janzen). Whether she felt happy or was blessed by the Lord is not the issue. The point is that her life was so extraordinary that she should be praised and others should try to be just like her. Her children agreed that she is the model of a blessed person.

Proverbs 31:30

This verse is a key verse in the passage. But it has several words that need clarification. The first is "charm" (hēn). In Proverbs 22:1, it had the meaning "favor" (e.g., NRSV). Here in 31:30, the parallel with "beauty" calls for the other meaning of "charm." Charm is a way of using a trait, such as physical appearance or friendliness, to attract people's attention. Charm can be "deceptive" (šeqer); it can give the appearance of something it is not. For example, a person can appear to be outgoing and friendly in public but be critical and cynical at heart. More than one marriage has ended because the charm on display while dating disappeared after the wedding ceremony was over.

"Beauty" is a quality that enriches life and adds enjoyment. Without it, life would be dull and boring. Beauty can be found in nature (a sunset or a snow-covered mountain), in human-made objects (a painting or a car), and in people. The advertising industry emphasizes beauty in all its promotions. Rarely do ugly people appear in ads.

But beauty has its faults. The most prominent is that it can be *hebel*. This is the Hebrew word translated "vanity" in Ecclesiastes (1:2, 14, etc.). It has four main meanings, depending on its context: something that (1) lacks substance (shallow, superficial), (2) is short lived (fleeting), (3) has no value (worthless), or (4) is "counter-rational" (senseless) (Fox 2004, xix). Here, the first meaning seems to be intended. Beauty has value, it may last a long time, and it is not senseless. However, it lacks substance. It is only skin deep. It does not reveal the true character of a woman. The author of 31:30 criticized this failing. Proverbs 11:22 expressed a similar thought.

The challenge the author presents to all young men is this: Would you rather have a wife whose only trait is charm and beauty, or would you rather have one who reflects the character of God? Which woman would be a good mother to your children, a steady support in times of crisis, and a faithful companion to the end of life? The author did not say a woman cannot be both beautiful and spiritual. He merely insisted that if you must choose one or the other, choose the woman of godly character.

This choice is like the one we considered in 22:1. There the choice was between wealth and a good reputation. As in that case, the author of 31:30 was not saying that one of the options was bad. Neither was he saying that we should not try to make the most of our appearance. He was simply saying that fearing the Lord was a much more important quality than beauty. In youth, beauty gets more attention and applause. But in the long run, only fearing the Lord gets a standing ovation from family and friends.

For many people, including me, that truth is encouraging. We were not all born with beautiful features; many of us have no hope of ever improving our appearance. However, we can all reverence and obey God. The author of this poem in Proverbs encouraged readers to do so. The mention of fearing the Lord reminded readers of the theme verse in 1:7. How appropriate to end the book with a phrase emphasizing again the theme of the entire book!

Proverbs 31:31

In the final verse the poet admonished the woman's community and every reader to give her the recognition she deserved. It should be of two types: "material and verbal" (Fox 2009, 899). We should reward such a woman materially for all her good deeds ("the fruit of her hands" [NRSV]). She was not to be just honored (NIV) or extolled (NJPS). She deserved to be repaid for her many acts of kindness and industrious behavior (NRSV).

The second clause encouraged vocal praise from those who had been recipients of her deeds (lit., "her works," personified). They were to praise her publicly ("in the city gates" [NRSV]). What can we learn from this virtuous woman in ancient Israel?

1. The Virtuous Woman Could Do It All

Proverbs 31:10-31 illustrates well how interpretations of some passages change over time. Up until the Reformation, this passage was usually interpreted allegorically. The woman represented the church. She was active both in the world and in the body of Christ. Since the Reformation, most scholars have opted for a literal interpretation—an ideal but real virtuous woman.

This woman, without a doubt, can do it all. She cooks (v. 15); sews (vv. 13, 19, 21-22, 24); shops, even with foreign merchants (vv. 13-14); educates her children (v. 26); manages her household (v. 27); runs a small business from her home (v. 24); offers help to the needy in her community (v. 20); even purchases new property and farms the land (v. 16). This is an extraordinary superwoman.

Because she is so ideal, a few scholars have seen her, not as a real person, but as a metaphor for Lady Wisdom (Clifford 1999, 274). Both women are strong and vigorous characters. Both are found at the city gates. Both are good teachers. Both bring good into people's lives and are extremely valuable to those who interact with them. Both are worthy of praise.

There are also some major differences. Lady Wisdom is not married and has no children. She has a house, but not a home. Her visits to the city involve confronting people about their folly and laughing at them when they reject her. She offers the rewards of long life, riches, and honor. She influences judges and rulers. Finally, she assisted God in the creation of the world.

The virtuous woman of 31:10-31 did none of these things. Thus it seems better just to regard her as a real human being, idealized to be completely exemplary. Her image has been photoshopped a bit. She provided young men considering marriage a picture of specific virtues they should look for in a wife. She demonstrated the importance of good virtues over good looks. For young women, she provided the opportunity to think about how their character might be improved.

2. The Virtuous Woman Knew the Value of Hard Work

Some people view work as only a means of making enough money to put bread on the table. On Friday at 5:00 p.m., their real life begins. In contrast, the virtuous woman of Proverbs 31 seemed to enjoy everything she did. It was not drudgery. Her work was good, "not just necessary" (Bartholomew and O'Dowd 2011, 122). Her every activity had a purpose. It contributed to the overall well-being of her family and her community. She knew she was making a positive difference in people's lives. This gave her the satisfaction she needed to stay active and avoid laziness (v. 27). Our work should do the same.

Further, this woman's work was always focused on her family. This woman did a lot of work outside her home—from shopping to selling, from buying land to planting a vineyard, and even helping the poor. But the center of her activities was always her home (Goldingay 2014, 154-55). She worked vigorously (v. 17), not for selfish gain, but to make her home function well (v. 27). Her family needed her to keep things running well and to keep God at the center of their home (v. 30).

3. The Virtuous Woman Saw the Importance of God in Her Life

Verses prior to Proverbs 31:30 laud the skills and vigorous endeavors of the virtuous woman. Verse 30 introduces readers to her spirituality. In addition to all her other excellent qualities, she was a devout woman of God. In fact, that was her most important characteristic and the main reason for her renown. This woman had many wonderful virtues, but her spirituality was the most important of all.

As mentioned earlier in our introduction to Proverbs, life was meant to be viewed from God's perspective. Humans were created to follow the order God embedded in the world. Even the ordinary, humdrum activities of life, such as cooking, sewing, and shopping, are part of God's plans for humanity. "For Proverbs there is no sacred-secular split" (Van Leeuwen 1997, 5:264). All of life has a spiritual dimension because all of life was created and ordered by God.

Conclusion

How should modern women view this ancient virtuous woman? Proverbs 31:10-31 presents an outstanding example of an ideal woman in ancient Israel. It does not apply practically to all women in all time periods. Not every woman aspires to all these virtues. Not every woman has the skills or personality to achieve all these roles. Modern women should recognize this as a list for a specific woman, time, and culture.

In addition, modern women should recognize that the list of skills and activities here is incomplete. The emphasis is always on what this woman *does*. Her reward is blessing, honor, and praise for her accomplishments. The passage says little about her relationship with her husband or children. She is hardworking, but is she loving? Is she caring? Is she romantic? We have no idea what motivates her work. Her privileged status undoubtedly gave her an advantage over most ordinary women of her time. The passage acknowledges her affluence; her family had servants, wore luxurious clothing, and operated a small business. The husband was a leading citizen in their town.

All women (and men) are unique. Every woman has a different income, different skills, different interests, a different personality, and a different level of health. Like the difference between Martha's and Mary's reactions when Jesus visited their home (Luke 10:38-42), some women are more task oriented and some more relationally oriented. This virtuous woman seems more like the first than the second.

Modern women need to recognize their own strengths and weaknesses and live confidently within them. The virtuous woman of Proverbs 31:10-31 provides an excellent model for some but not all women. A single mom caring for a disabled child and struggling to pay the rent might find the virtuous woman exhausting or depressing and not an ideal to which she would want to aspire.

Finally, a comment is in order about this woman's family circumstances. This woman was married with children. However, her family's situation was not the reason she was praised. It was her fear of the Lord.

Women today may be found in a variety of social relationships: single, divorced, widowed, married without children, married with children, and caring for grandchildren or parents. Every one of these women can live a successful life if she (1) fears the Lord (v. 30) and (2) cultivates, under God's guidance, achievable goals of character and behavior in her responsibilities to her family, to her friends and neighbors, to her coworkers, and to the world at large. When the fear of the Lord is foundational in all that a woman is and does, her worth is more than rubies or jewels. She is a pleasing daughter of God.

Possible Sermon Titles: "She Can Do It All, or Can She?" "A Woman Who Should Be Praised," "A Modern Example of Femininity?" "Who Can Find a Virtuous Woman?" "Worth More than Rubies" "An Ideal or Practical Example of Womanhood? Which Is It?" "A True Daughter of God"

X. ADDITIONAL SERMON IDEAS FROM PROVERBS

I did not set out to write this book to provide pastors or Bible teachers fully developed sermons or lessons. The sermon starters I offer here are not ready to be preached as they are, at any time or in every setting. They need to be developed and adapted to your personality and for your people. My illustrations are probably not the ones you will want to use in your church. But they may remind you of something from your personal experience that will be much more effective.

I hope my sermon starters provide useful examples of sermons or lessons you can make your own. Your congregation or class deserves to be exposed to this often-neglected part of the Christian canon of Scripture. This neglect is regrettable, but you can change that. The proverbs that were developed and passed on for centuries among the ancient people of God should not be forgotten.

It is my prayer that this book will challenge you to consider allowing the inspired wisdom of Israel's ancient sages to speak again to the people of God in our day. In case the preceding chapters were not enough, here are some further themes you could develop into sermons or lessons based on Proverbs.

The Importance of Knowledge

Proverbs 1:7, 22, 29-31; 2:5-6, 10; 3:20; 5:2; 8:8-10; 9:10; 10:14; 11:9; 12:1, 23; 13:16; 14:6-7, 18; 15:2, 7, 14; 17:27; 18:15; 19:2, 25, 27; 20:15; 21:11; 22:12, 17-21; 23:12; 24:3-7, 14; 28:2; 30:2-3

Making Plans for the Future

Proverbs 11:14; 15:22; 16:1, 3, 9; 19:21; 20:18, 24; 21:5, 18, 22, 30-31; 24:5-6, 27; 27:1

God's Judgment/Justice

Proverbs 2:7-9; 15:3, 11; 16:2, 8, 11; 17:3, 23; 18:5; 20:9, 11, 27; 21:2-3, 7; 22:8, 12; 24:10-12; 28:5; 29:26; 30:12

How to Treat the Poor

Proverbs 10:15; 13:8, 23; 14:20-21, 31; 15:25; 17:5; 18:11, 23; 19:4, 7, 17; 21:13; 22:2, 7, 9, 16, 22-23, 28; 23:10-11; 28:3, 27; 29:7, 13; 30:14

Guidelines for Leaders

Proverbs 6:7; 8:15-16; 12:24; 14:28, 34-35; 16:10, 12-15, 32; 17:2, 7; 19:10, 12; 20:2, 8, 26, 28; 21:1; 22:11, 29; 23:13; 24:21-22; 25:1-7, 15; 28:2, 15-16; 29:2, 4, 12, 14, 26; 30:29-31; 31:4

Dealing with Enemies

Proverbs 16:7; 17:13; 20:22; 24:17-18; 25:21-22; 27:6

REFERENCES

Aitken, Kenneth T. 1986. *Proverbs*. The Daily Study Bible. Louisville, KY: Westminster John Knox.

Anderson, Bernhard W. 1986. *Understanding the Old Testament*. 4th ed. Englewood Cliffs, NJ: Prentice-Hall.

Balentine, Samuel E. 2018. *Wisdom Literature*. Core Biblical Studies. Nashville: Abingdon.

Bartholomew, Craig G., and Ryan P. O'Dowd. 2011. *Old Testament Wisdom Literature: A Theological Introduction*. Downers Grove, IL: InterVarsity.

Bowes, A. Wendell. 2018. *Job: A Commentary in the Wesleyan Tradition*. New Beacon Bible Commentary. Kansas City: Beacon Hill Press of Kansas City.

———. 2021. *Consider My Servant Job: An Interpretive Guide for Preachers and Teachers*. Kansas City: Foundry.

———. 2024. *The Wisdom Literature*. Reading and Interpreting the Bible Series. Kansas City: Foundry.

———. 2025. *Half Empty: An Interpretive Guide to Ecclesiastes*. Kansas City: Foundry.

Brueggemann, Walter. 2019. *Preaching from the Old Testament*. Minneapolis: Fortress.

Childs, Brevard S. 1979. *Introduction to the Old Testament as Scripture*. Philadelphia: Fortress.

Clifford, Richard J. 1998. *The Wisdom Literature*. Interpreting Biblical Texts. Nashville: Abingdon.

———. 1999. *Proverbs: A Commentary*. The Old Testament Library. Louisville, KY: Westminster John Knox.

Collins, John J. 1980. *Proverbs, Ecclesiastes*. Knox Preaching Guides. Atlanta: John Knox.

Crenshaw, James L. 2010. *Old Testament Wisdom: An Introduction*. 3rd ed. Louisville, KY: Westminster John Knox.

———. 2017a. *Sipping from the Cup of Wisdom*. Vol. 1, *Exploring Diverse Paths of Research*. Macon, GA: Smyth and Helwys.

———. 2017b. *Sipping from the Cup of Wisdom*. Vol. 2, *Faith Lingering on the Edges*. Macon, GA: Smyth and Helwys.

Davis, Ellen F. 2000. *Proverbs, Ecclesiastes, and the Song of Songs*. Westminster Bible Companion. Louisville, KY: Westminster John Knox.

Farmer, Kathleen A. 1991. *Who Knows What Is Good? A Commentary on the Books of Proverbs and Ecclesiastes.* International Theological Commentary. Grand Rapids: Eerdmans.

Fox, Michael V. 2000. *Proverbs 1–9: A New Translation with Introduction and Commentary.* The Anchor Bible 18A. New York: Doubleday.

———. 2004. *Ecclesiastes: The Traditional Hebrew Text with the New JPS Translation/Commentary by Michael V. Fox.* The JPS Bible Commentary. Philadelphia: Jewish Publication Society.

———. 2009. *Proverbs 10–31: A New Translation with Introduction and Commentary.* The Anchor Yale Bible 18B. New Haven, CT: Yale University.

———. 2015. *Proverbs: An Eclectic Edition with Introduction and Textual Commentary.* The Hebrew Bible: A Critical Edition. Atlanta: SBL.

Freedman, David Noel, ed. 1992. *The Anchor Bible Dictionary.* 6 vols. New York: Doubleday.

Fritsch, Charles T. 1955. "The Book of Proverbs: Introduction and Exegesis." Pages 765-957 in vol. 4 of *The Interpreter's Bible*, edited by George Arthur Buttrick. New York: Abingdon.

Goldingay, John. 2014. *Proverbs, Ecclesiastes, and Song of Songs for Everyone.* Old Testament for Everyone. Louisville, KY: Westminster John Knox.

Gowan, Donald E. 1980. *Reclaiming the Old Testament for the Christian Pulpit.* Edinburgh: T. and T. Clark.

Hartley, John E. 2016. *Proverbs: A Commentary in the Wesleyan Tradition.* New Beacon Bible Commentary. Kansas City: Beacon Hill Press of Kansas City.

Horne, Milton P. 2003. *Proverbs, Ecclesiastes.* Smyth and Helwys Bible Commentary. Macon, GA: Smyth and Helwys.

Hunter, Alastair. 2006. *Wisdom Literature.* SCM Core Text. London: SCM.

Kidner, Derek. 1964. *The Proverbs: An Introduction and Commentary.* London: Tyndale.

———. 1985. *The Wisdom of Proverbs, Job and Ecclesiastes: An Introduction to Wisdom Literature.* Downers Grove, IL: InterVarsity.

Lambert, W. G. 1960. *Babylonian Wisdom Literature.* Oxford, UK: Oxford University Press. Reprint, Winona Lake, IN: Eisenbrauns, 1996.

Lichtheim, Miriam. 1973–2006. *Ancient Egyptian Literature: A Book of Readings.* 3 vols. Berkeley, CA: University of California Press.

Lodahl, Michael. 1994. *The Story of God: Wesleyan Theology and Biblical Narrative.* Kansas City: Beacon Hill Press of Kansas City.

Longman, Tremper, III. 2006. *Proverbs.* Baker Commentary on the Old Testament: Wisdom and Psalms. Grand Rapids: Baker Academic.

———. 2010. "Preaching Wisdom." Pages 102-21 in *Reclaiming the Old Testament for Christian Preaching*, edited by Grenville J. R. Kent, Paul J. Kissling, and Laurence A. Turner. Downers Grove, IL: InterVarsity.

McKenzie, Alyce M. 1996. *Preaching Proverbs: Wisdom for the Pulpit.* Louisville, KY: Westminster John Knox.

McLaughlin, John L. 2018. *An Introduction to Israel's Wisdom Traditions*. Grand Rapids: Eerdmans.

Miller, Patrick D. 2009. *The Ten Commandments*. Interpretation: Resources for the Use of Scripture in the Church. Louisville, KY: Westminster John Knox.

Murphey, Cecil. 2001. *Simply Living: Modern Wisdom from the Ancient Book of Proverbs*. Louisville, KY: Westminster John Knox.

Murphy, Roland E. 1998. *Proverbs*. Word Biblical Commentary 22. Nashville: Thomas Nelson.

Pauw, Amy Plantinga. 2015. *Proverbs and Ecclesiastes*. Belief: A Theological Commentary on the Bible. Louisville, KY: Westminster John Knox.

Perdue, Leo G. 2000. *Proverbs*. Interpretation: A Bible Commentary for Teaching and Preaching. Louisville, KY: Westminster John Knox.

———. 2007. *Wisdom Literature: A Theological History*. Louisville, KY: Westminster John Knox.

———. 2008. *The Sword and the Stylus: An Introduction to Wisdom in the Age of Empires*. Grand Rapids: Eerdmans.

Pippert, Wesley G. 2003. *Words from the Wise: An Arrangement by Word and Theme of the Entire Book of the Proverbs*. N.p.: Xulon.

Pritchard, James B., ed. 1969. *Ancient Near Eastern Texts Relating to the Old Testament*. 3rd ed. with supplement. Princeton, NJ: Princeton University Press.

Rad, Gerhard von. 1972. *Wisdom in Israel*. Translated by James D. Martin. Nashville: Abingdon.

Reyburn, William D., and Euan McGregor Fry. 2000. *A Handbook on Proverbs*. New York: United Bible Societies.

Schipper, Bernd U. 2019. *Proverbs 1–15*. Hermeneia. Translated by Stephen Germany. Minneapolis: Fortress.

Schloerb, Rolland W. 1955. "The Book of Proverbs: Exposition." Pages 765-957 in vol. 4 of *The Interpreter's Bible*, edited by George Arthur Buttrick. New York: Abingdon.

Scott, R. B. Y. 1965. *Proverbs, Ecclesiastes: Introduction, Translation, and Notes*. The Anchor Bible 18. Garden City, NY: Doubleday.

———. 1971. *The Way of Wisdom in the Old Testament*. New York: Macmillan.

Tobin, Thomas H. 1992. "Logos." Pages 348-56 in vol. 4 of *The Anchor Bible Dictionary*, edited by David Noel Freedman. New York: Doubleday.

Treier, Daniel J. 2011. *Proverbs and Ecclesiastes*. Brazos Theological Commentary on the Bible. Grand Rapids: Brazos.

Van Leeuwen, Raymond C. 1997. "The Book of Proverbs: Introduction, Commentary, and Reflections." Pages 17-264 in vol. 5 of *The New Interpreter's Bible*, edited by Leander E. Keck. Nashville: Abingdon.

Waltke, Bruce K. 2004. *The Book of Proverbs: Chapters 1–15*. The New International Commentary on the Old Testament. Grand Rapids: Eerdmans.

———. 2005. *The Book of Proverbs: Chapters 15–31*. The New International Commentary on the Old Testament. Grand Rapids: Eerdmans.

Weeks, Stuart. 2010. *An Introduction to the Study of Wisdom Literature*. T. and T. Clark Approaches to Biblical Studies. London: T. and T. Clark.

Westermann, Claus. 1995. *Roots of Wisdom: The Oldest Proverbs of Israel and Other Peoples*. Translated by J. Daryl Charles. Louisville, KY: Westminster John Knox.

Witherington, Ben, III. 1994. *Jesus the Sage: The Pilgrimage of Wisdom*. Minneapolis: Fortress.

Wolf, Earl C. 1967. "The Book of Proverbs." Pages 453-544 in vol. 3 of *Beacon Bible Commentary*. Kansas City: Beacon Hill Press of Kansas City.